Chinese Wildlife

A VISITOR'S GUIDE

Martin Walters

Photographs by
Heather Angel

www.bradtguides.com

Bradt Travel Guides Ltd, UK
The Globe Pequot Press Inc, USA

edition

I

First published February 2008

Bradt Travel Guides Ltd
23 High Street, Chalfont St Peter, Bucks SL9 9QE, England
www.bradtguides.com
Published in the USA by The Globe Pequot Press Inc,
246 Goose Lane, PO Box 480, Guilford, Connecticut 06437-0480

British Library Cataloguing in Publication Data
A catalogue record for this book is available from the British Library

ISBN-10: 1 84162 220 6
ISBN-13: 978 1 84162 220 0

Photographs
All photos taken by Heather Angel/Natural Visions (www.naturalvisions.co.uk),
with the exception of the following other Natural Visions photographers:
M & J Bloomfield (M&JB); Jeff Collet (JC); Richard Coomber (RC);
G & P Corrigan (G&PC); Doug McCutcheon (DMc); David Harrison (DH);
Sylvain Hellio (SH); Andrew Henley (AH); Gregory Guida (GG); Chris Newman (CN);
Anne Norris (AN); Paul Sawer (PS); Slim Sreedharan (SS); Ian Tait (IT);
Francesco Tomasinelli (FT); Jason Venus (JV); Michael Windle (MW)

Yangtze river dolphin (page 65): photo by Steve Leatherwood

Front cover Giant panda
Back cover Snow leopard
Title page (from top to bottom) Lotus; red panda; pied kingfisher (IT)

Maps Michael C Wood

Designed and formatted by Pepenbury Ltd
Printed and bound in India at Nutech Photolithographers

CONTENTS

AUTHOR

Martin Walters is a writer, editor and naturalist, based in Cambridge. He studied Zoology at Oxford University, and has had a lifelong fascination with birds, botany, natural history and conservation. His wide range of publications includes books on birds, flowers, trees, garden wildlife and travel. Martin has travelled to many parts of the world observing wildlife, and he has a particular interest in the natural history and culture of China.

PRINCIPAL PHOTOGRAPHER

Heather Angel, who took most of the photographs in this book, is a biologist and award-winning wildlife photographer. Since she first visited China in 1984, she has made many trips to photograph natural landscapes and wildlife. Her great passion is pandas and she has written three books about them. Heather has had two solo exhibitions of her work in Beijing in 1998 and 2003. She was President of the Royal Photographic Society from 1984–86 and has been a Special Professor at Nottingham University since 1994.

MAJOR CONTRIBUTORS

Prof. Wang Sung is Research Professor at the Institute of Zoology, Chinese Academy of Sciences, Beijing. An expert on mammals and conservation, he is one of China's leading zoologists and is actively involved in efforts to preserve the nation's biodiversity, having been awarded the 2003 Edinburgh Medal for his work in conservation. He founded the Biodiversity Working Group and works together with members from China and the international community on biodiversity conservation issues.

Dr Xie Yan is Director of the China Programme of the Wildlife Conservation Society and Associate Research Professor in the Institute of Zoology, Chinese Academy of Sciences, Beijing, as well as Director of the Interdisciplinary Research Promoting Centre and Secretary of the International Society of Zoological Sciences. Her special interests include biodiversity conservation, information systems, invasive species, protected area management, threatened species status assessment, vegetation restoration, biogeographic divisions of China and the Chinese mammalian fauna.

ACKNOWLEDGEMENTS

The author would like to give special thanks to Dr Xie Yan for providing the latest information on China's nature reserves and the status of rare and interesting animals and plants, and to Prof Wang Sung for writing the Foreword. He would also like to acknowledge the help of Heather Angel, whose splendid images adorn the pages of this new book, and who also wrote the section *Photographing Natural China*.

FOREWORD

In many countries, both 'developed' and 'developing', various guidebooks on local wildlife have been published. However, there is a distinct shortage of books about the wildlife of China. This is partly due to a lack of available information from field surveys. Surveys of Chinese mammals, for example, were mainly done by Western naturalists, from the mid 19th to the early 20th century. Field surveys by Chinese scientists began in the early 1950s, but unfortunately these were short-lived, being replaced largely by laboratory-based modern molecular biology.

As a result, detailed knowledge about Chinese wildlife is still lacking, and information about species diversity in Chinese reserves is often based on records dating back 30 or 40 years. Hence, there is a pressing need to update this information based on solid field survey and taxonomy, and there are likely to be more species yet to be discovered in China's diverse habitats and wild places. For example, recently a hedgehog species was discovered in the forests of Gaoligongshan Nature Reserve, Yunnan, although there had been no previous records for this region during the 19th and 20th centuries. This is just one example of the gaps in our knowledge of China's wildlife. The same is true also for other vertebrate groups, and still more so for invertebrates. There are doubtless many plant species awaiting discovery as well.

In China, wildlife conservation is a great challenge due largely to long-term over-harvesting and overuse, in part caused by a long history of tradition and entrenched unsustainable behaviour, such as hunting wildlife for food, and the uninformed use of rare and endangered species for traditional Chinese medicine (TCM). Over the years many mammals have been over-hunted for their fur, skeletons, meat, glands and derivatives, partly for use in TCM. A famous example is Père David's deer, an

Herd of Père David's deer running in the mist, Nan Haizi Milu Park, outside Beijing.

China's pageant of bird life includes such gems as this little green bee-eater. (GG)

endemic deer which was widely distributed in central and eastern China and which has been extinct in the wild for over 1,000 years, because of over-harvesting for its meat and antlers. The saiga in northwestern China has been hunted to extinction for its skin, meat and for parts used in medicine, especially its horns. The Mongolian gazelle, which used to be abundant, is now highly endangered. Other species, such as the south China tiger, have long been regarded as unwelcome or even pest animals, and were hunted to probable extinction, partly for their skins and skeletons. Meanwhile, musk deer (for musk) and pangolin (for meat and for scales), which used to be widely distributed in China, are also now highly threatened due to over-harvesting. Unfortunately, such animals are not given the same prominent status as more iconic species such as the giant panda. It is essential to increase knowledge of China's wildlife in order to encourage changes where there are such entrenched traditional views of wildlife.

For all these reasons, publishing a book such as this is both timely and urgent, partly to promote further fieldwork, conservation and ecotourism, and partly to increase public education and awareness.

This book is an introduction to Chinese wildlife, incorporating some of the latest data from Chinese experts. There is a need to promote continued co-operation between Chinese and Western scientists and amateur naturalists, and this book goes a step further towards promoting links between China and the international community.

Recently there has been much emphasis in China on international co-operation in the areas of tourism, trade and sport (notably in the case of the 2008 Olympic Games). As the environment becomes an ever more pressing issue worldwide, such a commitment must also be advanced in the areas of ecology and conservation. I hope that the reader will find this visitor's guide to be a useful addition to the existing publications.

WANG SUNG
Research Professor at the Institute of Zoology,
Chinese Academy of Sciences

LANDSCAPE, HABITATS AND PLANT LIFE

A wind-sculpted pine tree *Pinus hwangshanensis* looms out of the mist on Huangshan in Anhui Province.

GENERAL LANDSCAPE FEATURES

The landscape of China is hugely varied. The map opposite shows some of the major landscape features, such as the deserts of the north and northwest, and some of the main mountain ranges, as well as major cities. Also shown are the country's major rivers – the Yellow River (Huang-He) in the north, the Yangtze (Changjiang) flowing through central China, and the Pearl River (Xijiang) in the south. In the southwest two further major rivers – the Salween (Nujiang) and further east the Mekong (Lancang Jiang) – drain southeast from the Tibetan Plateau and then run roughly from north to south through the Hengduan Mountains and on through Yunnan. Almost parallel with these in southeast Tibet and north Yunnan is the Upper Yangtze (Jinsha Jiang). The Salween reaches the sea in Myanmar and the Mekong in Vietnam, but the Yangtze makes a number of sharp turns before flowing east right across China, to emerge eventually near Shanghai. The Yangtze thus forms a convenient natural border between northern and southern China. One other major river has its source in Tibet, this time in the southwest of the province. This is the Brahmaputra, called the Zangpo in China. It flows east along the Himalayan foothills in Tibet before turning sharply south to reach the sea eventually in Bangladesh.

On a very broad scale we can think of China as having three main sections. The west is dominated by the Tibetan Plateau, which lies at between 4,000 and 5,000m, rising to the Himalayan peaks in the south, with Mount Everest the world's highest mountain at 8,848m. The northwest is dominated mainly by deserts and grassland, with an altitude of between 500 and 1,000m, grading from very dry in the west, to semi-arid in the east. Finally, eastern and southern China holds most of the low-lying land, accounting for about 45% of the country and supporting 95% of the people. Unsurprisingly, the lowlands have been the most altered by people, and are for the most part intensively cultivated. For our purposes we have divided the country into eight regions, defined by a somewhat arbitrary combination of ecology and geography.

Tianchi is an alpine moraine lake within easy reach of Urumqi. (G&PC)

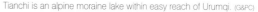

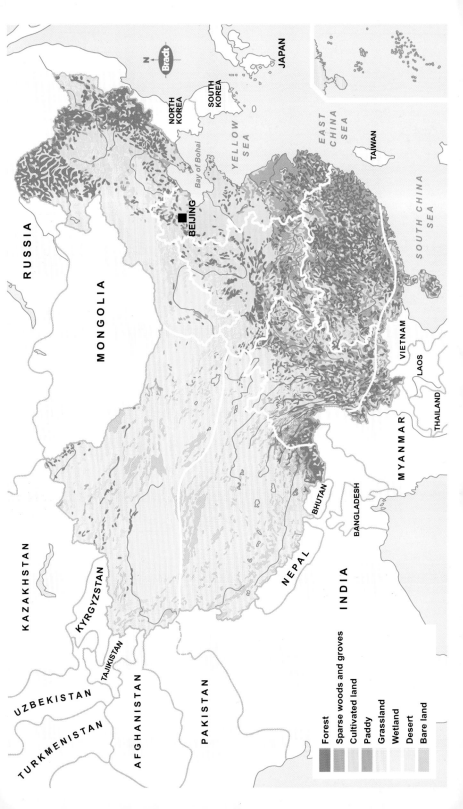

Clouds swirling around forested mountain peaks in north Yunnan.

HABITATS

China has a vast territory, with complex climates, varied geological and landscape types, a large network of rivers, many lakes and long coastlines. Such complicated natural conditions inevitably result in diverse habitats and ecosystems.

The terrestrial ecosystems can be divided into several types, including forest, shrubland, meadow, steppe, savanna, desert, tundra, high alpine communities and marsh, among others. The aquatic ecosystems may conveniently be classified as marine, rivers and lakes.

FORESTS

For a country which would naturally be extensively forested, the area covered by forest today is very small – only some 14% of the country, representing about 4% of the world's total forest area. Forest is rather unevenly distributed and the proportion of forest coverage ranges from 55% in some provinces to as little as 4% in others. Although much diminished in area, China's forests more than make up for this in their complexity and diversity, especially the mixed forests of the central and southern regions.

Forest types can be roughly divided into three categories: coniferous, broad-leaved deciduous, and coniferous and deciduous mixed. Within this broad classification more than 200 different forest types (formations) have been recognised, indicated by the dominant or co-dominant species, or by characteristic species in the tree-layer. Bamboo forests are a particular speciality and 36 types of this habitat alone have been described.

Coniferous forest

This is the dominant type of forest in the cold temperate zone, in the far northeast, bordering Russia. Fir, spruce, hemlock, pines and larches dominate in these northern forests, known as taiga.

There are also montane coniferous forests on many of the mountain ranges, even in the subtropical and tropical regions.

Temperate coniferous and deciduous broad-leaved mixed forest

This is mainly found in northeast China. These mixed forests typically feature Korean pine (*Pinus koraiensis*) with birch and other broad leaved trees.

Broad-leaved deciduous forest

This forest type is widely distributed over hilly areas and mid- or low-mountainous areas in the temperate, warm-temperate and subtropical zones. Historically, it is the natural vegetation of the warm-temperate zone and has been severely degraded and largely removed from most lowland regions. Deciduous oaks, beech and chestnuts feature in these habitats.

Broad-leaved evergreen forest

This type of forest is composed of many broad-leaved evergreen tree species and is characteristic of the subtropical region. These forests are typical for much of southern and southeast China, from Chengdu and Shanghai in the north, to Kunming and Guangzhou in the south. These are some of the richest of China's forests, with evergreen oaks, chestnuts and Chinese fir.

River and mixed forest in an alpine valley, Yunnan.

Tropical rainforest, Jianfengling NR, Hainan.

Tropical monsoon forest and tropical rainforest

Tropical forests cover a rather small area in southern China, occupying only 0.5% of the total area, but they host a staggering 25% of the total number of species in the country. These forests are mainly distributed in the southwest part of Yunnan Province, on Hainan Island and in southern Guangxi. They have been seriously depleted over the last half-century, and therefore protection of the remaining remnants is a very high priority for the conservation of biodiversity in China. Here, the forests are often dominated by tall trees of the dipterocarp family, and the undergrowth is frequently very lush and dense.

MEADOWS, STEPPES AND SAVANNAS

The dominant species in China's open countryside are mesophytes (plants that grow in conditions with average moisture) and perennial plants. These habitats can be divided into various types: typical meadows, saline meadows, marsh meadows and high-altitude cold meadows.

Steppes in China are dominated by perennial xerophytic herbs (those adapted to withstand dry conditions) and occur from temperate to tropical zones. Many types of steppe have been described, and these can be roughly grouped into: meadow steppe, typical steppe, desert steppe and high cold steppe.

Steppe habitats can be found in temperate semi-arid zones, such as the Qinghai-Tibet Plateau, and also in arid mountainous areas with dominant grasses such as feathergrass (*Stipa* spp.), fescues (*Festuca* spp.), *Aneurolepidium* and *Cleistogenes*, and also herbs such as wormwood (*Artemisia* spp.). The total area of temperate steppe in China is 315 million ha. Due to over-exploitation and over-grazing, about a third of the steppe regions have been severely or partially degraded.

Arid savanna in China can only be found in the xerothermic (both dry and hot) valleys in southern Yunnan and on some parts of Hainan Island. However, some tropical forests have become secondary savanna.

DESERTS

Desert covers a total of 20% of the landmass of China, and is mainly found in the northwestern part of the country. This habitat can be divided into four types, according to growth forms of the dominant plants, which are: tree desert, shrub desert, semi-shrub and small semi-shrub desert, and finally cushion-like small semi-shrub desert.

Napa Hai grassland, near Zhongdian in Yunnan.

Bactrian camel feeding in desert in Xinjiang.

The numbers of plants, animals and microorganisms in this ecosystem are relatively small, and the food chains within the ecosystem are simple. The dominant plants are drought-resistant species such as saxaul (*Haloxylon* spp.), Przewalski's ephedra (*Ephedra przewalskii*), *Zygophyllum xanthoxylon*, *Nitraria*, the tamarisk-like *Reaumuria* and winterfat (*Ceratoides*). Among the larger animals, lizards predominate, not only in species numbers but also in population size. Larger desert mammals include Bactrian camel and Asiatic wild ass, and the desert also supports many rodents including jerboas and gerbils. Przewalski's horse was also once found in these habitats; it has been extinct in the wild for years, but a reintroduction project is now under way.

In addition, there are many formations of tundra, alpine cushion-like and alpine mobile sand vegetation, covering relatively small areas.

WETLANDS

Wetlands in China extend over an area of 25 million ha and include some of the most biologically diverse and threatened ecosystems in Asia. China's wetlands are key habitats for endangered or endemic plants and animals, and they are also crucial staging and breeding areas for migratory birds, including many globally threatened species. In addition, there are 38 million ha of man-made wetland habitats comprising rice fields and other socio-economically important wetland areas. The 25 million ha of natural wetlands include 11 million ha of marshes and bogs, 12 million ha of lakes and 2.1 million ha of coastal saltmarshes, mudflats and shorelines. Approximately 80% (20 million ha) of China's wetlands are freshwater. Wetlands are distributed extensively in all regions of China, from the northernmost bank of the Heilongjiang River in the north, to Hainan Island and the islands of the South China Sea in the south; and from the coastline in the east to the arid northwest. The great variety of natural conditions in these different zones gives China's wetlands distinctive local characteristics. Some of the tropical coasts support mangrove swamps.

Freshwater ecosystems

Inland freshwater ecosystems are distributed mainly in the Qinghai-Tibet Plateau, Xinjiang and Inner Mongolia autonomous regions, Guizhou-Yunnan Plateau, Jianghan Plain and Sanjiang Plain. Twenty-two of China's many rivers are longer than 1,000km, and 2,848 of her lakes are larger than 1km². Many of China's rivers and streams are badly polluted and efforts are being made to introduce green technology solutions, though the damage already done is serious and long-lasting in many areas. The three-gorges dam project on the Yangtze is also likely to have severe effects on the ecology of the middle and lower Yangtze catchment, although the full consequences for the wildlife will not be known for some years.

Lakes in China are rich in aquatic biological resources and species. They provide habitats for phytoplankton, zooplankton, aquatic vascular plants and freshwater fish. About 690 species and subspecies of fish are endemic to China. Many lakes are connected with rivers with similar species composition. China is also one of the largest producers of freshwater aquarium fish in the world: of these, the silver carp, bighead and grass carp are quite well known in aquaculture.

Marine ecosystems

China's seas cover three climatic zones (warm-temperate, subtropical and tropical), and there are a number of coastal and marine ecosystems, such as coastal flats, estuaries, coastal wetlands, mangroves, coral reefs, marine islands and oceanic ecosystems.

Fallen trees under clear blue water in Five Flower Lake, Jiuzhaigou.

Mangroves at low tide on Hainan Island.

PLANT LIFE

The flora of China is vast – the country is home to about 31,000 species, or about an eighth of the world total. Compared with, for example, the 20,000 species of the US and Canada combined, this is indeed an impressive tally. This is partly explained by the fact that China is the only country in the world with long-lasting (though now very fragmented) connections between boreal, temperate, subtropical and tropical habitats. Many species therefore persisted in spite of the glaciations of the Ice Ages, by retreating to lowland or more southerly ice-free refuges, and then recolonising when warmer conditions returned. In much of Europe and North America, many ancient species were eliminated by these glaciations. Some examples of Ice-Age relict genera in China are *Cercidiphyllum*, *Ginkgo*, *Metasequoia* and *Pseudolarix*.

In the Cretaceous Period (about 135–66 million years ago) the Indian and African landmasses were separated from Eurasia by a large body of water, the Tethys Sea. At this point the land that was destined to become the Tibetan Plateau was actually part of the sea bed, and attached to the Indian landmass. Then in the Tertiary Period (about 66–2 million years ago) the Indian plate gradually closed the Tethys Sea and collided with the Eurasian plate, heaving the land up into the Tibetan Plateau and crumpling it to form the Himalayas, in a process (which is still under way) beginning some 40 million years ago. The Himalayas are relatively young for mountains, and only became the world's highest within the last 600,000 years.

In the early Cretaceous the main plants were the non-flowering gymnosperms – conifers, cycads, ginkgo and their relatives. During the late Cretaceous and early Tertiary, the flora was enriched by flowering angiosperms and gradually developed into the rich, diverse communities that may still be found in the more remote and undisturbed sites today.

Western plant collectors began to discover the riches of the Chinese flora in the later 19th and early 20th centuries, making expeditions to China, especially to the west and southwest, and bringing back botanical treasures for the gardens of Europe. The most famous of these were: George Forrest (1873–1932) from Scotland; E H ('Chinese') Wilson (1876–1930), Reginald Farrer (1880–1920) and Frank Kingdon Ward (1885–1958) from England; and Joseph Rock (1884–1962) from Austria. Forrest began visiting China in 1904, mainly to northwest Yunnan. He is best known for collecting rhododendrons (more than 300 new species), but also brought back camellias, magnolias, Himalayan poppies, gentians, primulas and lilies, many of which, such as *Primula forrestii*, were named in his honour.

One of the more remarkable features of the Chinese flora is that it holds a large proportion of the total number of species from several plant genera, for example 37% of *Fraxinus* (ash) species, 60% of *Ligustrum* (privet) species and 80% of *Syringa* (lilac) species.

China is also home to large numbers of plant species from very large and widespread families, such as the daisy family (Asteraceae), orchids (Orchidaceae) and grasses (Poaceae).

Plants in Chinese culture

Some 11,250 species of plant have been used medicinally in China, nearly 5,000 species are still used today informally, of which about 600 are commonly used in formalised traditional Chinese medicine (TCM). TCM shops offer herbal remedies for a bewildering range of complaints and illnesses. Nowadays Western medicine is investigating many traditional Chinese plants, seeking active compounds with pharmaceutical potential. One example is the wormwood *Artemisia annua*, which yields a drug that is effective against all strains of the malaria parasite. Another is *Trichosanthes kirilowii*, a member of the cucumber family endemic to China, which shows strong activity against HIV, the virus that causes AIDS.

The Chinese have used native plants for food and medicine for thousands of years; indeed to the Chinese these two are intimately connected and the distinction is sometimes blurred. Healthy eating results in a healthy body, and to some extent plant use in TCM overlaps with gastronomy, perhaps more so in China than anywhere else.

People have cultivated vegetables in China from as early as 8000BC and thousands of cultivated plants originate there, including yam, taro, rice, tea, soya bean, citrus fruits, cucumber, peach, apricot, and spices and medicines such as ginger, aniseed and ginseng. Rice, so typical and ubiquitous in China today, was probably first used for food and cultivated in southwest China and adjacent north Thailand around 7000BC. Soya bean, by contrast, hails from northeast China. First recorded around 1000BC, it is now grown across the rest of China and in other parts of southeast Asia.

In addition, China is the home of many of our familiar garden plants, now cultivated all over the world. Examples include camellias, cotoneasters, forsythias, gardenias, jasmines, magnolias, primroses, rhododendrons, azaleas and viburnums.

TREES

Although lowland China has been denuded of woodland over large areas, trees still have a central place in Chinese culture, and are often revered. Rare species such as ginkgo and fig trees are often planted at temples and other holy sites, and may be centuries old and very healthy. Some of the more remote mountains retain remnants of important original forests.

Conifers

Pines are fairly well represented in China. In the north and northeast the main species are the low-growing *Pinus pumila*, Scots pine (*P. sylvestris*) and Korean pine (*P. koraiensis*). In the southwest the Yunnan pine (*P. merkusii*) and Chinese white pine (*P. armandii*) are important, while the Chinese pine (*P. massoniana*) features mainly in the southeast. Firs (*Abies*), hemlocks (*Tsuga*), spruces (*Picea*) and larches (*Larix*) all feature in China's coniferous forests. Siberian fir (*Abies sibirica*) is a rare fir found in the northwest of the Altai Mountains of Xinjiang.

Dawn redwood (*Metasequoia glyptostroboides*) is rather a famous tree, and one of China's finest botanical treasures. This beautiful conifer has a restricted native range in Sichuan, Hubei and Hunan, on damp sites in mountain valleys between about 800 and 1,500m. Dawn redwoods are now widely planted in China and elsewhere, but this tree was only known from fossils until it was discovered in central China in 1948, where it persists in small numbers in the wild. Like larch, it is a winter-deciduous conifer, shedding its leaves in the autumn. Dawn redwoods grow to more than 40m.

Larches are important in the northern coniferous and mixed forests, where in some areas they colour vast swathes of the forest a brilliant yellow in autumn. Chinese larch (*Larix chinensis*) is found only in the Qinling Mountains of Shaanxi between 2,600 and 3,500m.

Chinese fir (*Cunninghamia lanceolata*) is a stately tree that grows wild in southeast China and is now widely planted. It has tough, rather spiny flattened leaves.

Mention must be made also of another remarkable conifer. This is the Cathay 'silver fir' *Cathaya argyrophylla*, a tree found only in Guangxi, Hunan, Sichuan and Guizhou, in about 30 different places, the main site being Laotizi in Jinfo Mountain on narrow mountain ridges at between 940 and 1,870m. The only species in its genus, it is most closely related to larch. Once much more widespread, its pollen has been found in Tertiary deposits in Europe and Asia. This remarkable tree has been dubbed the 'panda' of the plant kingdom because of its uniqueness and rarity.

Ginkgo (*Ginkgo biloba*) is perhaps China's most famous tree, familiar from gardens and for its medicinal properties, but rare in the wild in its native China. There are only a handful of sites where it is thought to be truly wild, in eastern China. Ginkgo is often dubbed a 'living fossil', a slightly misleading term referring to the fact that fossil specimens indicate that it has hardly changed over 100 million years. In fact there have been some changes – for example early ginkgos had more divided leaves. Like conifers and cycads, ginkgo belongs to a group of plants known as gymnosperms ('naked seeded'), which produce seeds but no flowers. This distinguishes them from the majority of contemporary plants, the flowering plants or angiosperms ('hidden seeded'). Individual ginkgo trees can be found in ancient gardens and outside temples, and some of these may be as old as 3,500 years. Extracts of ginkgo are used medicinally to treat various conditions and are commonly available from herbalists and pharmacies. Ginkgo fruits contain nuts, which are poisonous when raw, but the shells are used medicinally. The generic name of this ancient tree is derived from the Japanese word 'ginkyo' meaning 'silver apricot'. The leaves are also used in Western medicine.

Chinese yew (*Taxus chinensis*) is a small endemic tree growing between 1,000 and 1,200m in scattered sites across central China.

Broadleaved trees

China's broadleaved and mixed forests contain many species of tree from the oak/chestnut/beech family (Fagaceae), most notably oaks (*Quercus* and *Lithocarpus*), chestnuts (*Castanea* and *Castanopsis*) and beech (*Fagus*). There are also other familiar European genera such as lime (*Tilia*), maple (*Acer*), poplar and aspen (*Populus*) and planes (*Platanus*).

The fan-shaped leaves of the ginkgo are used in Western medicine.

Populus euphratica is a poplar from northern China, adapted to grow in desert and steppe regions. This hardy tree can withstand extremes of temperature – from -40°C to 45°C – and it produces beautiful bright coppery-orange autumn colours. *P. pamirica* and *P. pruinosa* are also found in Xinjiang.

Rather more unusual are the dove tree or handkerchief tree (*Davidia involucrata*), pagoda tree (*Sophora japonica*) and tulip tree (*Liriodendron chinense*). The dove tree takes its common names from the large white bracts (petal-like leaves) that open

Dawn redwood is a deciduous conifer that turns a reddish-brown in autumn.

The camphor tree produces an oil used in aromatherapy.

near the flowers in spring. These droop down at either side of the flowers, like the wings of a dove, or waving handkerchiefs. It is native to woodland in western Sichuan and Hubei, mainly in mixed forests between 1,250 and 2,200m. It was discovered by Armand David in 1869 and named in his honour. Pagoda tree is probably so named because of an association with Buddhist temples. It is a popular tree with pretty dangling spikes of creamy flowers, and is often planted in the west. Tulip tree is rare in the wild – it grows mainly in southern and central China, south of the Yangtze Basin, in mild, humid mountain broadleaf forests between about 900 and 1,800m. It is in the magnolia family and has large showy yellow-green flowers. The leaves are very distinctive in shape, looking rather like a mandarin's jacket; indeed it is sometimes called the mandarin jacket tree.

Hupeh rowan (*Sorbus hupehensis*) is a pretty tree from western China, with blue-green foliage and pinkish-white berries. It has bright red autumn colours. Another splendid tree now grown outside China is the princess tree (*Paulownia tomentosa*), found wild in central and western China. It has spectacular dangling clusters of purple foxglove-like flowers and large heart-shaped leaves. Its soft seeds were used for packing porcelain ('china') in the 19th century. This superb tree can often be seen planted in cities and alongside roads.

Manchurian walnut (*Juglans mandshurica*) is an interesting tree found wild in mixed forests of the northeast – in Inner Mongolia, Hebei, Henan, Shanxi and Shaanxi on sunny hillsides between about 400 and 1,000m. The European walnut (*J. regia*) is also found in China, but is rather rare in the wild and restricted to the western Tian Shan in Xinjiang. It is however widely cultivated, mainly in western China.

Cinnamon trees (*Cinnamomum*) are not uncommon in the forests of central and southern China, and are also planted along streets. Their leaves and bark have an aromatic fragrance. These are evergreen trees in the laurel family that grow to about 20m. Another typical tree, also in the laurel family, is *Litsea*. Litseas have yellow flowers and grey, rather scaly bark. There are a number of species in China's mixed forests.

Magnolias are well known in cultivation and they produce beautiful large flowers – usually white or pink – that appear before the foliage. Southern China is a centre for this genus (and the related genera *Manglietia* and *Michelia*), but many species are threatened in the wild – in fact more than half of the world's 245 species are under threat. They are cut for timber and also used medicinally. One of the most impressive is *Magnolia campbellii*, which has large pink flowers with outer spreading petals. A much rarer species is Baohua or zen magnolia (*M. zenii*), known from a single population at the type locality in the Baohua Mountain, Jiangsu Province. Like most magnolias, it produces large, fragrant flowers. Another rare magnolia is *M. phanerophlebia*, also known from only one area, with a tiny population of fewer than 250 trees. This species has great horticultural potential with its pale apricot-coloured fragrant flowers set off against its deep green foliage. Sadly, both are threatened by habitat loss. *M. sargentiana*, from Sichuan and Yunnan, has light pink flowers, while those of *M. sinensis* and *M. wilsonii* are white. Sichuan manglietia (*Manglietia szechuanica*) grows in forests of central Sichuan between about 1,300 and 2,000m; it has pinkish-white flowers, while the flowers of *M. martinii* and *M. wilsonii* are a pretty pale yellow.

Top Dove tree flowers have large white bracts.
Above Wilson's magnolia was discovered by E H Wilson in 1904.

In the far south of the country there are some splendid trees in the precious remaining tracts of tropical forest. Prominent amongst these are members of the dipterocarp family (Dipterocarpaceae), of genera including *Parashorea*, *Shorea* and *Vatica*. Another impressive tall rainforest tree is *Tetrameles nudiflora*, the sole member of its family, which has large, flanged buttresses towards its base. Some of these trees can grow into real giants – well-grown individuals can tower as tall as 50m, forming the tallest rainforest canopy. Arrow-poison tree (*Antiaris toxicaria*) is another tall tree capable of reaching 40m, from the monsoon forests of Yunnan, Guangxi and Guangdong. Its highly poisonous sap has been used in some places to coat arrowheads.

SHRUBS AND HERBS

A discussion of China's many flowering shrubs and herbs can seem almost like a gardener's guide, as so many species and genera of popular garden flowers have their wild origin in China. Indeed Western botanical gardens, parks and private gardens would be severely impoverished were one to remove all the Chinese constituents. Among shrubs for example, all the following well-known genera are Chinese or contain important garden species originating from China: *Berberis, Buddleia, Camellia, Cotoneaster, Daphne, Forsythia, Jasminum* (jasmine), *Ligustrum* (privet), *Magnolia, Pyracantha* (firethorn), *Rhododendron, Syringa* (lilac) and *Viburnum*. The list of familiar garden annual and perennial flowers of Chinese origin is also a long one, and includes many members of the following genera: *Aster, Anemone, Azalea, Begonia, Clematis, Cypripedium, Delphinium, Dendranthema, Geranium, Hypericum, Iris, Lilium, Paeonia, Papaver, Polygonum, Potentilla, Primula* and *Rosa*.

Butterfly bush

Many species of *Buddleia* originate from China, most notably *B. davidii*, which is a deciduous shrub growing to about 3m. Its panicles of fragrant purple flowers are famously attractive to butterflies and other insects. This species is native to the highlands of west and central China, where it grows on thin soils in rocky sites such as alongside rivers. It has been introduced to many other parts of the world where it has often become established as an invasive weed, albeit a pretty one, as well as an extremely popular garden plant.

Camellias

This genus (*Camellia*) has about 200 species, and the genus is native to China, Japan and Indo-Malaysia. Tea is produced from varieties of *C. sinensis*, but many other species are grown for their ornamental flowers, and many splendid garden hybrids are now available. Yellow-flowered species include *C. flava, C. nitidissima* and *C. tonkinensis*. Golden camellia (*C. nitidissima*) is sometimes called the Queen of camellias, and has bright golden flowers. It is found wild only in wet forests in south Guangxi. An interesting species is *C. omeiensis* with deep red flowers, which occurs only around Emei Shan in Sichuan. *C. grijsii* from southeast China has large pure white flowers.

Orchids

With about 1,100 species, China is extremely rich in orchids. Yunnan is the best province for them, with more than 530 species in about 100 genera. Of these, the slipper orchids (*Cypripedium*) are particularly well represented. *C. henryi* from central and southwest China has green flowers with a pale yellow inflated lip. One of the most impressive is *C. tibeticum* from Tibet, Yunnan and Sichuan. This delightful species has bright purple-red flowers. *Pleione yunnanensis* is another beautiful orchid. It produces delicate pale violet flowers on single leafless stalks and grows in the mountains of the southwest, between 2,000 and 2,800m.

Almost all China's plant groups seem to have been used in traditional medicine and the orchids are no exception. This has had a severe effect on the population of

The slipper orchid *Cypripedium tibeticum* flowers in summer at Napa Hai.

the widespread saprophytic orchid *Gastrodia elata* in many areas. The underground tubers contain several active compounds and the species has been used for more than 1,500 years in herbal medicine to treat arthritis, vertigo, numbness, to improve blood circulation and also as an aphrodisiac. A rather unusual orchid-like plant grows in the deserts of northern China, between 150 and 1,500m. This is *Cistanche deserticola*, a parasitic broomrape species that gains its nourishment from the roots of saxaul bushes. Most of the plant remains below ground, but it sends up tapering flower spikes that can be up to 1.6m tall. These have dense clusters of yellowish-white pink-edged flowers and look very strange indeed poking straight up out of the desert sands. This species is also valued as a natural medicine and is said to improve kidney function, among other effects.

Peonies

Beloved of gardeners in the West, peonies (*Paeonia*) are an important part of the Chinese flora. Many wild species were brought into cultivation, and have given rise to the range of garden cultivars and hybrids available today. Such is the wealth of peonies in China that there are even dedicated peony tours available, and these flowers feature in many Chinese parks and gardens. *Paeonia rockii* is a famous tree peony from which many cultivars have been produced. Another fine peony is *P.*

delavayi, which has purple-red flowers and golden anthers. It grows wild in Tibet, Sichuan and Yunnan, on sunny slopes between 2,300 and 3,700m. *P. suffruticosa* grows in mountain forests of central China, and has large white or pink flowers, while *P. lutea* is a yellow-flowered species. *P. veitchii*, with deep pink flowers, grows mainly in subalpine shrubland and grassland, and this and *P. suffruticosa* are also grown for their pharmaceutical properties, for example in the Sichuan Basin.

Primulas

There are about 300 wild species of these familiar garden plants (*Primula*) in China, out of a world total of about 500, and more than 200 are endemic. They are especially diverse in the mountains of the southwest. Chinese primrose (*P. sinensis*) is a tall perennial with lobed leaves and delicate pink flowers. It is native to west central China. *P. faberi* from Sichuan and Yunnan has a basal rosette of leaves from which grow bright yellow flowers on long stalks. *P. forrestii* is another impressive yellow-flowered primula from southwest China. *P. latisecta* grows only in Tibet. It has deeply lobed leaves and terminal clusters of purple flowers. *P. purdomii* produces fine umbels of bluish-purple flowers; it grows in the mountains of Qinghai, Gansu and Sichuan. Another mountain species is the orchid-like *P. vialii*.

Top Paeonia rockii or Rock's peony has deep red spots on the inner petals.
Left Primula vialii or Chinese pagoda primrose grows in wet places.

Rhododendron yunnanense grows in mountain forests.

Rhododendrons

Plant hunters will definitely want to see some of China's wonderful rhododendrons (*Rhododendron*), and dozens of rhododendrons now grown in European gardens originate from China, especially from Sichuan, Yunnan and Tibet. China has about 650 of a world total of 850 species. Many of these are endemic and the hills and mountains of the southwest are the best sites to visit, especially in Sichuan and Yunnan. Rhododendrons vary in size from small shrubs to tall species with a tree-like stature. All have leathery leaves and impressive clusters of the rather showy flowers that make them so sought after by gardeners. The shrubby species are often important components of the shrub layer in subalpine forests, where they add glorious splashes of colour to the undergrowth. On more exposed high-altitude slopes above the forests, low-growing species such as *R. nivale* (purple) are important, as is the creeping *R. forrestii* (dark red). Another impressive species is *R. rubiginosum* from high-altitude (2,600–3,800m) forests of west Yunnan and southwest Sichuan, which grows to 6m tall. This striking species produces copious clusters of beautiful rose-pink flowers.

Of the taller species, the tree rhododendron (*R. arboretum*), with deep blood-red flowers and growing to 10m, is one of the finest. Local species include *R. beesianum* with bell-shaped pink flowers, and the endemics *R. calophytum* (white and pink flowers) and *R. davidii* (pink-purple). Mainly white-flowered species include *R. liliiflorum*, *R. hunnewellianum* and *R. yunnanense*, while *R. triflorum* from southeast Tibet has rather delicate pale yellow fragrant flowers. The yellow snow rose (*R. chrysanthum*) is rather a local species growing in open, rocky sites, such as in the Changbaishan reserve in Jilin Province in the far northeast. This low-growing species with creamy-white flowers is highly prized as a medicinal plant, extracts being used to treat arthritis.

The wingthorn rose *Rosa sericea* var. *pteracantha* grows on Emei Shan

Roses

Roses (*Rosa*) have been cultivated in China for centuries, and a number of Chinese species have been especially important introductions to the West. One of the main characteristics that Chinese roses offered rose-breeders was repeat flowering. The red-flowered *R. chinensis*, probably native to Sichuan, was introduced at the end of the 18th century. *R. odorata* var. *gigantea* (= *R. gigantea*), also known as the wild tea rose, and *R. rugosa* also grow wild in China and have contributed much genetic diversity to rose breeding. The former was introduced to Europe in 1888 and grows wild in southwest China. It is a tall plant with large pale yellow flowers. The latter has purplish-red flowers and grows wild along the coasts of Liaoning and in Jilin and Shandong. In fact over 90 species of rose are native to China (from a world total of about 150), with a high proportion of endemics. The so-called 'China rose' is actually a complex of species and hybrids, evolved over centuries of cultivation in Chinese gardens. Another popular garden rose from west and central China is Banksian rose *R. banksiae*, a climbing rose with yellow or white flowers. The bark of the roots of the latter is used in tanning. *R. webbiana* is a pretty pink-flowered Himalayan rose that is fairly common in parts of Tibet.

Taccas

Members of this tropical genus (*Tacca*) have highly unusual flowers that are pollinated mainly by flies. They are tuberous herbs related to lilies but classified in a family of their own, containing two species in this single genus. *Tacca chantrieri* grows in mountain forests of central and southern China, up to about 1,350m, in wet valleys and along streams. The individual flowers are surrounded by four purple-brown bracts, and up to 24 thin, ribbon-like bractlets droop down from the flowerhead. *T. integrifolia* has white bracts and purple drooping bractlets that may be almost 60cm long. These flowers look very odd – rather like spiders suspended over the forest floor.

Black tiger lily flower (*Tacca chantrieri*) with whisker-like bractlets.

The chusan or Chinese windmill palm produces golden flowers.

Palms

As well as introduced coconut palms in coastal sites, there are some interesting native palm species found in tropical regions. These include the tall Chinese fan palm *Livistona chinensis*, and the fish-tail palm *Caryota* with elegant splayed array of leaves. *Caryota urens* grows in the limestone forests of Yunnan where it may be as tall as 25m. It has long, fern-like doubly divided compound leaves clustered at the top of the stem. The rich sweet sap is fermented into an alcoholic drink (toddy) in some regions. Much smaller, at only about 1m, is the endemic dwarf windmill palm *Trachycarpus nana*, which is found only in mixed forests of Yunnan at around 2,000m. Taller, to about 15m, is the related Chinese windmill palm (*T. fortunei*), which is one of the hardiest of all palms, and is native to central and eastern China. It has been grown in China for centuries for its fibres, which are used to make ropes, sacks and coarse cloth.

In Xishuangbanna, the leaves of the palm *Corypha umbraculifera* (native to India, Sri Lanka and Malaysia) are used by the Dai people as paper for religious inscriptions (sutras), and holy books made of these leaves are still used in the temples. Another name for the Hinayana Buddhism practised by the Dai is 'Palm Leaves Buddhism Sutra Culture'.

The paper is prepared by boiling the leaves with tamarind and citrus fruits to bleach them, then scrubbed with sand, dried and pressed, before being pierced and fastened together between wooden panels. Rattans (*Calamus*) are specialist clambering palms that grow up forest trees in the rainforests of the south. Their strong fibres and stems are used to make ropes and furniture.

Others

The beautybush (*Kolkwitzia amabilis*) is an attractive shrub with twin pink or purple flowers, endemic to central China and is the only species in its genus. It grows on sunny slopes.

Chrysanthemums (*Dendranthema*) have a special place in Chinese culture. They have long been regarded as special, and many cultivars have been produced, first yellow, then later white and purple-flowered forms, derived mainly from the wild *D. indica*. This is also one of many important medicinal plants, chrysanthemum tea being regarded as beneficial and effective against fever and sore throat.

Many species of Clematis (*Clematis*) are native to China, including *C. armandii*, *C. chinensis*, *C. delavayi*, *C. montana* and *C. orientalis*.

Potted chrysanthemums in a Suzhou garden.

Cotoneaster (*Cotoneaster*) is another popular garden plant, several species of which (including *C. acutifolius*, *C. horizontalis*, *C. integrifolius* and *C. lacteus*) originate in China. Many have decorative pink or red berries, beloved of birds, and fine autumn leaf colour.

Dragon's blood tree (*Dracaena cambodiana*) is a woody, small tree with rosettes of linear leaves and a rare plant from the southwest of Hainan. It has long been used in traditional medicine to improve blood circulation, and it is now being cultivated to preserve the wild stocks.

Saxaul (*Haloxylon ammodendron*) is a small deciduous tree or shrub with grey bark and scaly leaves, characteristic of steppe and semi-deserts of northern China (Inner Mongolia, Gansu, Xinjiang and Qinghai).

FRUITS, VEGETABLES, SPICES AND MEDICINALS

Hundreds of fruits, vegetables and other useful plants are grown in China. We include here a selection of the more interesting or unusual. Most of these are found wild in China or have wild relatives there.

Apple (*Malus*)

Wild forms of apple still grow in certain valleys in the hills of western Xinjiang, and these may be part of the ancestry of cultivated apples. *Malus sieversii* for example is found on slopes at around 1,500m and is one of a number of wild species. It has white blossom and small greenish-yellow fruits.

Arrowhead (*Sagittaria sinensis*)

This aquatic is grown in China, and harvested for its starchy corms, which are usually sliced and fried. The name comes from the arrowhead-shaped aerial leaves.

Overview of South Sichuan Bamboo Sea from a cable car.

Bamboo

Many species of bamboo (*Phyllostachys* and *Dendrocalamus*, among others) are harvested for their edible shoots, which are cut when they first emerge then boiled to remove the bitter taste. Bamboo forests are found in several parts of China, notably in the provinces of Fujian, Jiangxi, Zhejiang, Hunan, Guangdong, Sichuan and Anhui. In some areas, they are cropped on a regular rotation, both for their culms and shoots. Bamboos provide a wide range of useful products, from poles for scaffolding and building, to water pipes, food and medicines. Split culms are also bound together to make 'Venetian' blinds, and even the offcuts from this process are not wasted, being turned into kindling or toothpicks. They are also commonly grown as garden plants, adding structure and grace, as well as green colour throughout the winter. There are important bamboo gardens and collections at Hangzhou, Nanjing, Guangzhou, Chengdu and Anji, among other places. Common garden forms include golden-stemmed bamboos such as *Phyllostachys aureosulcata*, the dark purple *P. nigra*, Buddha's belly (*Bambusa ventricosa*) and the square-stemmed *Chimonobambusa quadrangularis*.

Bulbs, leaves and roots

A leafy form of white-stalked celery (*Apium graveolens*) is popular in China. It has a strong flavour, and the leaves and stems are normally cooked together. The bulbs of various species of lily (*Lilium*) are eaten in China and taste rather like parsnips when boiled. Chinese chives (*Allium tuberosum*) and rakkyo (*A. chinense*) are commonly grown in China. The blanched flat leaves of the former are cooked as a vegetable, while it is mainly the shallot-like bulbs of the latter that are eaten. The Chinese small onion (*A. fistulosum*) has hollow leaves and very small bulbs. It is commonly eaten in China, often being added to give extra flavour to fried vegetables. Taro (*Colocasia esculenta*) is an ancient tropical food plant that has been cultivated for centuries in India and south China. The potato-like tubers are cooked and eaten, and the leaves are also edible. Yam (*Dioscorea alata*) has large tubers that are nutritious and sweet, and also easily stored.

Lily bulbs for sale as food.

Cabbages and other vegetables

The complex cabbage family (*Brassica*) has many examples from China. Chinese mustard (*B. juncea*) is grown for its spicy-flavoured leaves. Pak choi (*B. rapa* subsp. *chinensis*) has been grown for centuries in China and plays a central role in many cuisines there, and increasingly abroad. Well known also is the celery cabbage, more often called Chinese leaves (*B. rapa* subsp. *pekinensis*), a sturdy, crisp form with a slightly mustard-like flavour.

Bitter cucumber (*Momordica charantia*) is native to tropical Asia and is eaten in China. Its fruits have a warty texture and a bitter flavour. Chinese artichoke (*Stachys affinis*) is an unusual mint relative native to China. It is grown for its swollen edible tubers, which are usually boiled.

Nearly all cultivated lettuces are derived from the wild lettuce (*Lactuca sativa*). In China, a variety known in English as celtuce (alternatively as asparagus lettuce or Chinese stem lettuce) is popular – this is *L. sativa* var. *augustana*. It produces swollen stems, which are sliced and often then stir-fried.

The wax gourd (*Benincasa hispida*), also known as winter melon, is a vegetable that has been cultivated for thousands of years in China. It is usually either stuffed, like a marrow, or used in pickles.

Citrus fruits

Citrus fruits (*Citrus*) originated in China and other parts of southeast Asia, from a handful of native species, of which *C. reticulata*, the mandarin, is the main ancestor from China. The other main ancestors are *C. maxima*, the pomelo, *C. medica*, the citron and *C. aurantifolia*, the lime. It is thought that all other citrus fruits are derived from these species, although the origin of some hybrids is lost in the mists of time, orange, *C. sinensis*, being one such example. One rather unusual citrus fruit is the large-fruited pomelo or Chinese grapefruit, *C. maxima*. This is larger than a grapefruit, pale green when ripe, and has thick soft rind and quite sweet flesh. It is commonly grown in southern China. An interesting and very rare citrus, *C. hongheensis*, grows in the mountains of southern Yunnan.

Ginger (*Zingiber officinalis*)
Both the stems and roots of ginger are regularly used in Chinese cuisine and this is a widespread crop in tropical and subtropical areas. Galangal (*Languas galanga*) has similar rhizomes to ginger and is used as a spice, mainly in south China.

Ginseng (*Panax ginseng*)
One of the world's most famous medicinal plants, ginseng is a perennial herb related to ivy. It has whorls of leaves and umbels of flowers that produce bright red berries. Ginseng is found mainly in northwest China in mountain forests between 400 and 1,000m. The fleshy tap root is the main source of medicines, used as a stimulant and to treat a variety of ailments. Over-collection of wild ginseng has seriously depleted this species.

Pepper (*Capsicum anuum*)
This and a number of other species originate in Central and South America, but some are also widely grown in China. They vary from sweet to very hot, the hottest usually (but not always) being the smallest. The unrelated Sichuan pepper is a famous hot spice from western China.

Plum and other fruits
Wild relatives of plums and peaches (*Prunus*) also grow wild in parts of northern China. One species, also well known as a garden plant in the West, is the cherry plum *Prunus cerasifera*. This is a many-branching small tree, growing to about 8m tall, with small white flowers and dark green foliage. Cherry plum grows in parts of Xinjiang, between 800 and 2,000m. Another wild species is Mongolian peach *P. mongolica*, from Inner Mongolia, Ningxia and Gansu, which has small peach-like fruits.

The fruits of longan (*Dimocarpus longan*), a tropical evergreen tree, are rather like lychees with sweet flesh. It grows wild in the forests of Yunnan, Hainan, Guizhou, Guangxi and Guangdong, below about 800m.

Chinese gooseberries (*Actinidia chinensis* and *A. chrysantha*) are unusual woody climbers with oval, furry fruits, now popular the world over. The flesh inside the fruit is green and rather acidic. Both species originate in southern China.

Radish (*Raphanus sativus*)
In the West we tend to think of radishes as (usually) small, round and bright red, but in China there are different forms, usually with long, thick white, green or purple roots that are sliced and cooked, often in soup.

Donkey cart selling radishes in Kashi (Kashgar) Bazaar.

Rice (*Oryza sativa*) and other grains

The staple grain of China, rice is central to life across the country and China is the world's largest producer. Different varieties are grown in different regions: in the south the main form is subsp. *indica* (hsien), while in the north the main type is subsp. *japonica* (keng). In the warm south the rice-growing season lasts from March right through to September. There are hundreds of traditional cultivars of rice, suited to local conditions and with different characteristics and flavours. However, many of these are now being lost and replaced by higher-yielding hybrids, threatening the valuable genetic diversity of the traditional forms. The traditional races are often better suited to the local conditions and are also more likely to be resistant to the pests of the area concerned. Common wildrice, *Oryza rufipogon*, grows wild in southern China, medicinal wildrice, *O. officinalis*, is found naturally in Guangxi, Guangdong and Hainan, and warty wildrice, *O. granulata*, is another wild species from Yunnan, Guangdong and Hainan. All three of these are important sources of genetic diversity and have been used in breeding commercial rice varieties.

Buckwheat species (*Fagopyrum esculentum* and *F. tataricum*) are widely grown in China. In the polygonum family, they bear small grains that are ground into a nourishing flour. Originally from Mexico, maize (*Zea mays*) is widely grown in China.

Top Rice terraces ready for harvest.
Right Buckwheat field in flower.

The sacred lotus is revered by Hindus and Buddhists.

Sacred lotus (*Nelumbo nucifera*)

This beautiful water plant, often wrongly called a water-lily, is well known for its large, elegant pink flowers and round, waxy floating leaves. Less well known is its value as a food plant: the rhizomes are cooked either fresh or pickled, the seeds roasted and even the young leaves used raw or cooked. It is easy to cultivate and many aquaculture pools in lowland China have sections devoted to lotus beds.

Soya beans help lower cholesterol levels.

Sichuan pepper (*Zanthoxylum simulans*)

This bush is the source of the very hot spice used in Chinese cuisine, especially in Sichuan Province where it is widely cultivated.

Soya bean (*Glycine max*)

This is a staple of Chinese food, being grown for oil, and used in many other ways, most notably for dofu (tofu). The wild soya bean (*Glycine soya*) is a widespread annual herb with purplish pea flowers and flat pods. It grows mainly in the Yangtze Basin and is a useful source of genetic diversity for soya bean breeding.

Tea (*Camellia sinensis*)

This genus is famous for many species with attractive flowers, but this particular species is noteworthy as the form that produces tea. The plant is native to southern Yunnan and Hainan, as well as other parts of southeast Asia. It is an evergreen tree or shrub, growing to between five and 20m tall, with rather rough oval leaves and white, fragrant flowers. Tea was being drunk in China as long ago as the time of Confucius (about 500BC), and by the Tang Dynasty (AD618–906) it had become firmly established as the national beverage. In those early days dried tea was moulded and pressed to form bricks that could be easily transported, and such brick tea can still be seen and purchased to this day. Later on, other methods came into fashion, using different times of picking, and different treatments including a period of fermentation. Black tea passes through a fermentation phase, green teas are generally unfermented, while oolong tea is partially fermented. The variety of different teas now available, especially in China, is quite staggering, and connoisseurs of tea now rival those of wine for their degree of detailed knowledge and expertise.

Water chestnut

Two unrelated plants (*Trapa natans* and *Eleocharis dulcis*) go under this name, and both are widely eaten in China. Incidentally, this neatly indicates the value of using scientific names. The first is a floating aquatic with spiny, hard fruits containing edible (when cooked) seeds; the second is a plant in the sedge family and grown like rice. It produces crunchy sweet corms, which are eaten either raw or cooked.

MORE THAN PANDA FOOD

Bamboo in China is not just the essential food of giant pandas, it is also central to traditional Chinese life and society. Bamboo features in Chinese painting, poetry and also in cuisine – its influence is seemingly everywhere, and it has been used by people in China for about 5,000 years. Even the physical properties of the bamboo plant are regarded as mirroring ideal human attributes: bamboo is simultaneously strong and flexible, offering reliable support, yet also bending to accommodate when required. Bamboo also symbolises modesty, gentleness and serenity.

Bamboos grow wild in many parts of China, most notably in the mixed subtropical forests of south-central regions, and there are more than 400 species. Although most prominent in the warmer southern regions, some bamboos grow as far north as Beijing, and from sea level right up to 3,800m in Sichuan and Tibet.

Bamboos of the genus *Fargesia*, especially the endemics *F. ferax* and *F. spathacea*, are important in the diet of giant pandas. These bamboos, often called umbrella bamboos, grow between 2,000 and 2,800m, mainly in the mountains of Sichuan.

In a number of such areas, local people have used bamboo and harvested the culms and shoots over many centuries. This has resulted in the gradual development of almost pure stands of certain bamboo species by targeted 'gardening' of the forests. The end product is a 'bamboo sea' of tall bamboo forest made up of fairly even-aged stands of tall culms. These are then harvested on a strict rotation to give a crop of poles, while a proportion of the fresh shoots are gathered as food. The most important commercial bamboo is undoubtedly mosu (mao zhu) bamboo *Phyllostachys pubescens* (= *P. heterocycla* var. *pubescens*), which is also almost as important in the timber industry as *Pinus massoniana* and Chinese fir.

Mosu bamboo covers about 3.5 million ha, or about 3% of China's total forest area. Bamboo grows faster than any other plant, and this species can grow nearly

120cm in 24 hours, and 24m in 50 days. One of the most famous sites for mosu bamboo is Changningzhuhai NR (Changning Bamboo 'Sea') in Sichuan. Another is the Anji area southwest of Shanghai.

Moso bamboo forest in Anhui.

Anji County, not far from Shanghai, lies in the foothills of the Tianmu Shan. Here the locals have extended the natural pockets of bamboo into vast swathes of secondary bamboo forest, which now clothe the mountain slopes. The bamboos here are cropped and used for poles and a wide range of other products, including edible shoots. This is a sustainable harvest which supports many of the local people. Much of the original mixed forest has been converted over a long period of time into these 'forest-gardens', involving several thousand years of production.

Anji County covers some 1,800km², has half a million inhabitants, and is about 73% covered by forest, with about 6% of the natural broadleaf forest protected. The concept for development here is very 'green', with natural products such as bamboo, silk and tea being generated alongside developing ecotourism. Each village has a quota for bamboo collection. Medicinal plants are also gathered from the bamboo groves (about 30 species are involved) and the orchid *Gastrodia* is actually cultivated within the forest. Although Anji is something of a pioneer, this ecological approach to forest exploitation is becoming more common in China, and is environmentally friendly. The products from bamboo include timber for building, furniture and handicrafts, plywood, charcoal, scaffolding (even in big cities), shoots (fresh, dried or processed), bamboo juice, bamboo beer and vinegar.

One unusual bamboo is *Qiongzhuea tumidissinoda* from Yunnan Province. This species has very prominent nodes and is usually known as 'walking stick bamboo', or Qiong Zhu. The latter, and also its generic name, come from the Chinese 'Zhu' meaning 'bamboo'. Known in China since the Han Dynasty, some 1,200 years ago, it has often appeared in Chinese art. Walking sticks made from this species were exported from China along the Silk Roads to India and Persia and beyond, yet the plants and their location in China remained a well-kept secret, and the species was only described and named scientifically in 1980. Not only are the culms used for walking sticks and for making other handicrafts, the pink shoots, which grow early in the year, are crisp and delicious, and large quantities are eaten fresh or dried, and they are also exported. Growing under broadleaved evergreen forest in the mountains between the edge of the Yunnan Plateau and the Sichuan Basin, from 1,600 to 2,900m, walking stick bamboo can withstand a temperature range of -10°C to 29°C, with annual rainfall of 1,100 to 1,400mm. The uses of this bamboo make it a highly valuable species, but loss of its natural habitat and over-harvesting, especially of new shoots, has put it in jeopardy. Deforestation of much of the natural habitat of this species in Yunnan and Sichuan provinces has led to its decline.

MAMMALS

Snow leopard

There are roughly 580 species of mammal in China, of which more than 100 are endemic and about 40% are threatened. Destruction of habitat, combined with over hunting for food and for medicine, has taken its toll on China's mammals, and some have dwindled in number to the point of near or even total extinction. There is, thankfully, some evidence that a new awareness of conservation is beginning to reverse this trend, though for some of the most threatened, notably the south China tiger and the Yangtze river dolphin, it may already be too late.

Reintroduction programmes are proving successful with some species, such as Père David's deer and Przewalski's horse. Key populations of these and other charismatic mammals, such as the giant panda, are now effectively preserved within reserves. As with China's vegetation and plant life, the mammal fauna shows similarities with that of northern Eurasia, with a fascinating admixture of southern, subtropical and tropical species adding to the interest as one moves south.

Compared with east Africa for example, mammals are not so easy to see in the wild in China. This is partly because many species are secretive and mainly nocturnal, and partly because the majority are restricted to dense forest habitats. Another reason is that generations of excessive hunting have reduced the density of many mammal species. Watching mammals is a very different skill from birdwatching, and those keen to do so may need to familiarise themselves with clues like footprints, droppings or feeding remains. Often the only way visitors to China are able to see native wild mammals is by visiting a zoo – often not a pleasant experience, as the conditions in which they are housed can be shocking.

CARNIVORES

Carnivores include cats, dogs, bears and pandas, and also weasels, otters and civets and their relatives. Most either feed exclusively on meat or include a high proportion of meat in their diet. Bears, however, are omnivorous and consume a wide range of food, including smaller mammals, fish, fruits and seeds. The highly specialised pandas are mainly (though not exclusively) vegetarian, feeding mostly on bamboo. Overall, carnivores are quite well represented in China, but many of the larger species are threatened and are now rare.

Cats

Four distinct subspecies of tiger (*Panthera tigris*) are (or were) found in China and all were formerly much more widespread. The Amur (Siberian) tiger (*P. t. altaica*) is the largest, measuring up to 3.75m from its head to the tip of its tail and weighing more than 200kg. The others are the much smaller south China tiger, (*P. t. amoyensis*), the Indochinese tiger (*P. t. corbetti*) and the Bengal tiger (*P. t. tigris*). The latter two occasionally enter China in southwest Yunnan and southeast Tibet. The Amur tiger can still be found in the forests of northeast China, towards the borders with Russia and North Korea, where it seems to be holding its own following major conservation efforts.

The south China tiger is probably now extinct in the wild.

Snow leopard on snow. Note the long, thick tail.

The story of the south China tiger is not a happy one, however. Once found across a wide belt of central and eastern China, this is the smallest and rarest of China's subspecies. It also has distinctly different markings, with broad, widely spaced stripes. Scientists believe that this race is closest to the ancestor of all the existing tiger subspecies. Its historical range included the lowlands, but unfortunately this is also China's most heavily populated region. In a sadly familiar story, it has long since been driven out of the lowlands into the forests and scrub of the hills and mountains.

These wonderful animals have been hunted almost to extinction, partly for their pelts and partly for their body parts, which regrettably continue to be used in traditional Chinese medicine. In 1993 China banned domestic trade in all tigers and derived body parts, but poaching is still a problem, as is the illegal importing of tigers and their parts from India. Tiger organs and body parts, including teeth, bones and penises, continue to fetch high prices on the black market. They are used to treat many ailments including rheumatism, and they are also said to act as an aphrodisiac.

In the 1940s there were thought to be at least 4,000 south China tigers, but by

1980 the numbers had dwindled to a mere 200. Between 1988 and 1990 there were reliable reports of tigers from scattered locations in southeast China, notably from Chebaling (Guangdong), Mangshan, Hupingshan and Zhangjiajie (Hunan), and from Wuyishan (Fujian), so it is just possible that a handful of wild tigers may still roam in some of these wilder sites, but seeing them, or even proving that they still exist, is virtually impossible. In 1995 the Chinese Ministry of Forestry indicated a wild population of fewer than 20, and no wild tigers have been seen by officials in more than 20 years. It is thus quite probable that this beautiful cat is already extinct in the wild. Detailed field surveys were undertaken in 2001 and 2002 in eight reserves in five provinces, but sadly found no trace of the tiger. Interviews with locals came to the same conclusion: extinction has either already occurred, or is imminent. There is a tiny captive population,

Leopard cats are superb swimmers. (SS)

but all individuals are inbred, which may jeopardise any reintroduction plans.

The snow leopard (*Uncia uncia*) is one of the most charismatic of all China's cats, partly because it is a beautiful creature with soft, subtly patterned fur, but also because it inhabits some of the most inaccessible and impressive mountain terrain – the exposed rocky slopes of Tibet and several other mountain ranges. Individual ranges cover many miles and so the chances of spotting a snow leopard, even where they are still known to occur, are pretty small. Most people will only ever see one in

The lynx is a long-legged cat, with huge paws. (SS)

a zoo, or as a pathetic pelt for sale. Illegal trading in the valuable skins is a problem for this splendid species and many are killed every year, but China still has an estimated population of about 2,000, representing half the global total. Snow leopards prey mainly on wild sheep and goats. In many areas the numbers of natural prey have declined, mainly through hunting, and this has forced snow leopards to take the occasional sheep or goat from shepherds' flocks. This has led in some cases to reprisals from the farmers, further reducing the numbers of snow leopards.

Leopards (*Panthera pardus*) are quite widely distributed in China, although much reduced in numbers in most places, and very hard to spot. This cat is highly adaptable and is found in habitats ranging from high mountains to dense forest. Until the 1990s leopards could even still be found in coastal Fujian, but they have been driven into ever more remote and highland sites. One of the rarest forms is the Amur leopard (*P. p. amurensis*), still found in the far northeast, for example in the Changbai Shan, where probably no more than 50 individuals survive.

Another large cat is the clouded leopard (*Neofelis nebulosa*), a mainly tropical and subtropical forest species, still found in some sites in southern China, including Hainan. There are recent records of this beautiful cat from Chebaling (Guangdong) and Shiwandashan (Guangxi). Clouded leopards are powerful stealth hunters, with large canine teeth, and feed on a range of prey including monkeys, birds and even small deer. They have particularly attractively patterned fur, which has led to their being hunted for their pelts.

China also has several smaller cats of the genus *Felis*. The lynx (*Lynx lynx*), familiar from Europe, is found across central and northern China, notably in Tibet and Mongolia, in a range of habitats, including forests and also high mountain plateaux. The Asiatic golden cat (*Felis (Catopuma) temminckii*) is about twice as large as a domestic cat and has short, rounded ears and may be golden, brown or grey.

The red fox has a distinctive white tip to the tail.

The wolf hunts as part of a pack.

It inhabits forest, mainly in southern China and Tibet. The leopard cat (*Prionailurus bengalensis*) is a beautifully spotted species, the size of a domestic cat, and is found across much of China. Sadly, it is often hunted for its fur and is now rare. The marbled cat (*Pardofelis marmorata*) is another attractive species, this one restricted to moist tropical forest. The Chinese mountain cat (*Felis bieti*) is endemic to China, mainly in east Qinghai and northern Sichuan. It has pale yellowish fur and a short tail. Pallas's cat (*F. manul*) is a small, solitary cat found in steppe regions such as the Tibetan Plateau.

Dogs

Both the wolf (*Canis lupus*) and red fox (*Vulpes vulpes*) are very widespread in China. The wolf is an important element in the ecology of the mountains and forests of the west and north, where there have been signs that it is on the increase. Elsewhere, centuries of persecution have reduced wolf numbers considerably, to the point of extermination in some parts of the country. Like snow leopards, wolves are affected by decreases in the populations of some of their natural prey species, such as wild sheep. This has led in turn to incidences of wolf attacks on domestic sheep and goats and consequent culling by herdsmen.

The Asian wild dog or dhole (*Cuon alpinus*) was once widespread, but has declined dramatically although it can still be found in Tibet and possibly also in nearby regions. Asian wild dogs resemble small wolves, but have reddish fur. The strange, squat-bodied raccoon dog (*Nyctereutes procyonoides*) has also declined, partly due to trapping for its thick fur, though it is also widely farmed for this purpose.

Sun bears have very long tongues for capturing termites. (SS)

Bears

The largest of China's bears, the brown bear (*Ursus arctos*) is widespread, particularly in northern forests, but also in parts of Qinghai and Tibet. The Asiatic black bear (*U. thibetanus*) is commoner, and is found locally in the mountain forests of western Yunnan Sichuan and on Hainan, among other places, but also in the northeast. It is smaller than the brown bear and has a distinctive pale V-shaped patch on its chest. The even smaller sun bear (*Helarctos malayanus*) inhabits subtropical and tropical forests in southern China, mainly in Yunnan, Guangxi and Guangdong. The sun bear also has a pale chest marking, but is much smaller than the black bear. Bears in China have long been persecuted and killed for their body parts (including bile), which are used in many traditional medicines. This practice, combined with habitat loss and general disturbance, has sadly reduced wild bear populations considerably.

The Asiatic black bear uses trees to sharpen its claws.

Giant panda mother with five-month-old cub at Wolong.

Giant panda (*Ailuropoda melanoleuca*)

Everybody's favourite cuddly toy, instantly recognisable and the symbol of global conservation as the World Wide Fund for Nature's emblem, the giant panda is undoubtedly China's most famous animal. Despite huge efforts at conservation it also remains one of the rarest mammals, though in recent years things are looking more hopeful. The giant panda's strongholds are the mixed mountain forests of west and central China, where it is increasing, albeit painfully slowly. There are still over 1,000 of these beautiful and endearing creatures in the crescent of mountain ranges that runs from west Sichuan across to south Gansu and south Shaanxi provinces. The most recent surveys (published in 2004) revealed that the total population stands at about 1,600, well up from the estimated 1,100 in the 1980s. While this may be partly due to more detailed and

Giant panda showing black stripe across back linking black forelegs.

accurate field techniques, the picture is nonetheless encouraging, with reduced poaching levels, combined with the establishment of more reserves, and very importantly, the creation of 'panda corridors' connecting the string of panda reserves so that genetic mixing can be encouraged to reduce inbreeding. The main threats to these marvellous animals are deforestation and illegal poaching, mainly outside the protected areas.

Sometimes classified in a family of its own, although now usually included in the bear family, giant pandas are unusual in many ways. Their black and white fur is highly distinctive, they feed almost exclusively on the fresh leaves and shoots of bamboo, and each front paw has a special extra 'thumb', actually a digit-shaped wrist bone evolved for handling bamboo culms. In order to get enough nourishment, pandas have to eat for up to 14 hours each day. However, they do sometimes eat meat if they come across it, to supplement their monotonous vegetarian diet.

As pandas feed extensively on bamboos, they have special adaptations to their teeth, gut and forepaws to accommodate this diet. Every 30 years or so, bamboos flower almost simultaneously over large areas and, after flowering and seeding, the mature plants die. Giant panda populations are jolted by sudden food shortage. Some animals starve, some survive on the reduced supply of bamboos that fail to flower and others migrate out of their valleys in search of new areas where the bamboos at lower altitudes or in further valleys have not yet flowered. Such behaviour also increases the genetic diversity of the panda population and so is beneficial to the long-term survival of the species. The problem in recent decades has been that extensive habitat fragmentation has made such dispersal much more difficult, resulting in a higher mortality amongst pandas.

Female giant pandas make dens in hollow trees or rock clefts where they have their babies.

The giant panda sits or lies down when feeding in order to conserve energy.

Giant pandas are found only in west and central China, mainly in a series of protected reserves, some set up especially to preserve this fascinating threatened species. Most of the sites are in Sichuan Province, to the west and north of Chengdu, in the following mountain ranges: Min, Qionglai, Xiangling and Liang. The Min Mountains overlap into southern Gansu Province where there are also pandas, and the other main sites are in the Qinling Mountains in Shaanxi Province, southwest of Xi'an.

There are now about 50 panda reserves, up from 13 just 20 years ago, with 36 of these in Sichuan. The most famous and largest is Wolong, not far from Chengdu, where there is also a panda museum and breeding centre. Saving the giant panda is a major challenge for China, and the animal has become a recognised symbol of Chinese wildlife and conservation efforts. Pandas usually give birth to twins, but normally only one survives. The breeding centre removes both of the new-born pandas from their mother and rears them in incubators until they are big enough to be returned to their mother and then safely raised. They also have a programme for acclimatising the young pandas gradually to the wild and releasing them. But this is not as easy as it sounds, and there have unfortunately been fatalities with released pandas coming into conflict with established wild pandas. It is hoped that the release programme will eventually be able to boost the wild population, perhaps by releasing some animals into suitable habitats that do not already have wild pandas, but it is by no means certain that this will be successful, and it is far better to protect and link areas of existing wild panda populations so that they can recolonise fresh habitats themselves.

BEAR OR RACCOON?

The relationship of the giant panda to other mammals has been the subject of debate ever since its existence became known in the West in 1869, discovered by French missionary Père Armand David. It was first named as a kind of bear, in the genus *Ursus*, but later re-named in its own genus, *Ailuropoda*. Although it is distinctly bear-like in appearance, it has many features that set it apart from bears, notably its very specialised diet and the special wrist bones that function as a pseudo-thumb, enabling it to grip bamboo shoots. It also resembles the red panda, which has generally been classified in the raccoon family, and both pandas have specialised teeth for crushing bamboo. So the question remains: is the giant panda a bear, a raccoon, or something else quite unique? This debate has continued for decades, with the giant panda being variously classified in the bear family (Ursidae), the raccoon family (Procyonidae), and even placed in its own family (Ailuropodidae).

The giant panda is a taxonomic puzzle.

Modern DNA studies have recently given general support to the idea that the giant panda is indeed a type of bear and this is how it is now classified. In fact it most probably represents an early divergence from the bear line, becoming highly specialised yet retaining an overall bear-like appearance. The similarities between the giant and red pandas are then most probably the result of convergent evolution, having evolved separately in these two species as an adaptation to a diet of mainly bamboo.

Interestingly, an earlier form of the giant panda has recently been discovered in China. From a skull two million years old, scientists have established that this was in fact a pygmy giant panda, about three feet long. It has been named *Ailuropoda microta*. This small ancestor was already adapted for a bamboo diet and seems to have been very similar to the modern giant panda, except for its size.

Red pandas spend a lot of time up trees

Red panda (*Ailurus fulgens*)

The red (lesser) panda is a cute, raccoon-like mammal with attractive red-brown fur, a banded tail and dark and white badger-like facial markings. Like its larger and more famous 'cousin', it feeds largely on bamboo, and so it is mainly found in areas where bamboos are common in the forest undergrowth, normally between about 1,500 and 5,000m. It also eats fruits and leaves and climbs well, spending more of its time in the trees. Like the giant panda, the red panda also has special adaptations of its paws and digestive tract to enable it to grasp bamboo stems and digest them. It often spends up to 13 hours each day searching for food and feeding. Primarily a Himalayan species, in China it is found mainly in Sichuan, Tibet and Yunnan. Though commoner than the giant panda, there may be as few as 5,000 left in China, so it is also endangered and worthy of strenuous conservation efforts. Habitat loss and hunting for its pelts are major threats to this beautiful animal. In some areas red panda pelts are made into traditional headgear and even sold to tourists, a practice now illegal and, one hopes, on the decline.

Otters, civets and other small carnivores

China has many small carnivores, including weasels and otters, and civets and their relatives. In addition to the common otter (*Lutra lutra*), there are also the smooth-coated otter (*Lutrogale perspicillata*) and the Oriental small-clawed otter (*Amblonyx cinereus*). Otters are also persecuted for their fur, especially since (surprisingly) otter skins form part of the Tibetan traditional dress, and all the species are threatened and now rare. The smooth-coated otter is the largest, and has a very flattened tail. The Oriental small-clawed otter is mainly found in southern China, especially near and at the coast. It uses its sparsely webbed front paws to catch and manipulate its prey – mainly crustaceans and shellfish. Civets are also found in many of China's forests. These mongoose relatives are cat-like slimline predators of smaller mammals and birds, although they also eat fruit and insects, and other invertebrates. The masked palm civet (*Paguma larvata*) inhabits southern forests. It is widely eaten in southern China (as are many other wild animals), and came to be suspected of spreading the infectious disease SARS, after which it became the subject of a cull. The Indian civet (*Viverra zibetha*) is a larger, more widespread species, mainly in southern China. Owston's palm civet (*Chrotogale owstoni*) is a rare species from southern Yunnan and southwest Guangxi. The chunky, bear-like binturong (*Arctictis binturong*) is related to civets, and lurks in the dense southern tropical forests of Guangxi and Yunnan, while the spotted linsang (*Prionodon pardicolor*) is another rare inhabitant of central and southern China's forests.

Otters often stand on their hind legs for a higher viewpoint. (JV)

HOOFED MAMMALS

Hoofed mammals, otherwise known as ungulates, are divided into two categories according to the arrangement of their highly specialised toes (hooves). Most belong to the even-toed group (order Artiodactyla) and this includes camels, pigs, deer, and the bovids – cattle, sheep, antelopes, gazelles and relatives. The other group, the odd-toed ungulates (order Perissodactyla), contains horses and relatives.

Pigs

Wild pigs (*Sus scrofa*) are widespread across China, found in all habitats except for deserts and high mountains. They are especially fond of mixed woodland, and sometimes emerge to root about in cultivated land.

Wild pigs foraging at dusk.

Bactrian camel (*Camelus bactrianus*)

The Bactrian camel, ancestor of the domestic two-humped camel, is now rare in the wild, being restricted to a few sites in the deserts of northwest China and adjacent Mongolia. Wild Bactrian camels were previously found across the deserts of southern Mongolia and northwestern China, and into Kazakhstan. Years of persecution have reduced the species to fragmented populations, three in northwest China and one in Mongolia. The largest population is currently found in the Gashun Gobi Desert (Lop Nur) in the Xinjiang Uighur Autonomous Region. Areas of the Gobi and Gashun Gobi Desert where the Bactrian camels that remain are protected by the Great Gobi Reserve in Mongolia which was established in 1982, and by the newly established national reserve 'Lop Nur Wild Camel Reserve' in China. Both the Chinese and Mongolian governments have agreed to protect this trans-boundary migrating species.

Back from the brink, the 26 Eld's deer left on Hainan Island in 1976 have increased to 1,600.

Deer

Reindeer (*Rangifer tarandus*) and moose (*Alces alces*) are northern species that are found mainly in the far northeast, near the border with Russia. Moose may also be present in the Helan Shan in north central China, which, if confirmed, would make this the most southerly site for this species. More special to China is the white-lipped deer (Thorold's deer) (*Cervus albirostris*). Endemic to China, it lives in high-altitude alpine steppe grasslands between 3,500 and 5,200m in northern Tibet and Qinghai, making it the world's highest-living deer. The attractively spotted and white-rumped sika deer (*C. nippon*), by contrast, is an eastern species, found mainly in grassland and forest margins in Jiangxi, Anhui and Zhejiang. Eld's deer (*Cervus eldi*) is found only on Hainan in China, while sambar (*Cervus unicolor*) is another southern species found on Hainan and also in mainland China. Tufted deer (*Elaphodus cephalophus*) is a small deer of central China's subtropical mountain forests, notably the Qinling Mountains. Père David's deer (*Elaphurus davidianus*) is a sturdy large deer endemic to China, and originally found on the eastern plains. Like the wild horse, it became extinct in the wild, but is now being reintroduced. The Chinese water deer (*Hydropotes inermis*) is well named as it prefers wet areas such as rivers, lakes and reedbeds, mainly in southeast China.

The very small, dog-sized muntjacs (*Muntiacus*) and the tiny mousedeer (*Tragulus javanicus*) are small deer that are found mainly in forests in the south, such as in Xishuangbanna. The Indian muntjac (*Muntiacus muntjak*) has a wide range in southern China, while the endemic black muntjac (*M. crinifrons*) is found mainly in western Zhejiang and south Anhui. A third species, Reeves's

Male Chinese water deer have protruding canines.

The lesser mousedeer is a tiny hoofed mammal. (SS)

muntjac (*M. reevesii*) is another endemic from east China and Taiwan. Incidentally, this is the species that has established itself so readily in England. Muntjacs communicate by means of abrupt dog-like barks. The lesser mousedeer (*Tragulus javanicus*) is the world's smallest deer, being only about the size of a rabbit. The four species of musk deer (*Moschus*) are also found in China. The strange-scented secretions of the musk gland have long been used in traditional medicine, and also in the perfume industry, and these small deer have therefore been hunted down the years for these trades.

PÈRE DAVID'S DEER

This rare deer is the subject of a fascinating story. It is endemic to China, native to marshy habitats in the north and east where it used to roam in reedbeds and swampy grassland, especially in areas subject to regular seasonal flooding, such as in the lower Yangtze valley, and also in certain coastal marshes. It is well adapted to such conditions, swimming well and spending long periods in the water, feeding on grasses, reeds and other waterside vegetation. It is an approachable deer, and this may well have been part of the reason for its demise, combined with its slow rate of reproduction with just a single calf per birth the norm. Large, elegant and rufous-brown, it is a splendid animal with distinctive antlers that sweep backwards with a long rear branch. Its head is elongated and slender with big eyes and small pointed ears, and the tail is long and tipped with a black tuft.

Père David's deer became extinct in the wild in the early 1900s, mainly because of over-hunting and habitat loss, with the last known wild specimen being shot in 1939. Luckily, a captive herd was maintained by the Emperor at Nanhaizi Park in Beijing and it was here that the deer was spotted by missionary Père David, who realised it was new to science and arranged for skins to be sent to Europe. These were used to make a formal description of the species. Sadly, the Chinese herd eventually perished, but by then several deer had been sent to Europe, and another captive herd was established at Woburn Abbey in Britain. Between 1985 and 1987, the Duke of Bedford then donated some of this stock back to China, in three groups. These animals were introduced to Milu Park in Beijing, to Sishou in Hubei and to Dafeng in Jiangsu. Happily, these herds are still thriving, and releases, both deliberate and accidental, have helped to strengthen the population and about 2,500 are now living wild again in China.

Père David's deer has backswept antlers and lives in swamps.

Goats and sheep

Caprids or goat-antelopes comprise wild sheep, goats and their relatives, and there are several species of this group of sturdy horned mammals in China.

Blue sheep (bharal) (*Pseudois nayaur*) are the commonest. They are typical of the Himalayas on mountain slopes between about 3,000 and 6,000m, while the splendid and much rarer Argali (Marco Polo) sheep (*Ovis ammon*) is found in Tibet and also in the northern mountains. Argali is the largest of all wild sheep, with massive curled horns up to almost 2m long and 50cm in circumference. Ibex (*Capra ibex*) found mainly in the mountains of northwest China also has large horns, though scimitar-shaped. The Himalayan tahr (*Hemitragus jemlahicus*) lives in small herds in forested hills in southern Tibet, between about 3,000 and 4,000m. This animal's horns are short and its body is protected from the cold by thick skin and dense, chestnut-coloured fur. The short-horned and dark-coated Himalayan serow (*Capricornis sumatraensis*) occurs in central China on steep, rocky habitats. The related goral is sometimes divided into three species: Himalayan goral (*Nemorhaedus goral*); Chinese (long-tailed) goral (*N. caudatus*); and red goral (*N. baileyi*). The latter has reddish fur and has a limited range in the mountains of western Yunnan (notably Gaoligong).

Probably the most interesting of China's goat-antelopes is the somewhat mysterious, large-headed takin (*Budorcas taxicolor*). This strange bovine is found in

The blue sheep or bharal is a mountain animal, occurring in Tibet.

mixed forests, marshy grassland and alpine pastures in certain mountains of western China, notably in western Sichuan, southeast Gansu and south Shaanxi, usually between 1,500 and 4,000m. It has long, shaggy fur, often almost golden in colour, and it is this coat that may have given rise to the legend of the golden fleece, brought back from afar by Jason in the Greek tale. In summer, takin graze on mountain slopes, then descend into the lower-altitude forests for the winter. They browse mainly on shoots, bamboo leaves, grass and bark.

The chiru (Tibetan antelope) (*Pantholops hodgsonii*) is not a true antelope, but is probably more closely related to sheep and goats. Native to the Tibetan Plateau and northern India, its numbers have been severely depleted mainly through hunting for its fine wool, which is woven into highly prized (and high-priced) 'shahtoosh' shawls. The wool of the chiru is regarded as the finest and many thousands of these magnificent animals have been slaughtered to feed this lucrative trade, and at least three

The takin has an attractive golden coat

chiru are killed to make just one shawl. Chiru live in large herds between about 4,000 and 5,500m, and graze mainly on grasses and lichens. Perhaps the inclusion of the chiru as one of the mascots for the 2008 Beijing Olympic Games will help heighten awareness of the perilous state of this magnificent animal.

Gazelles

True gazelles are represented in China by four species. Goitered gazelle (*Gazella subgutturosa*) and the endemic Przewalski's gazelle (*Procapra przewalskii*) live mainly in the steppes and semi-deserts of the northwest, while Mongolian gazelles (*P. gutturosa*) are found in the grasslands of Inner Mongolia. Only about 500 wild Przewalski's gazelles remain. The main threat to them is fencing built by locals to protect rangelands. These have blocked migration routes and increased vulnerability to predators. The fourth species, the charming Tibetan gazelle (*P. picticaudata*), lives mainly on the Tibetan Plateau, in high-altitude steppe and grassland, usually in small groups of three to five. All the gazelle species are threatened by poaching.

Saigas (*Saiga tatarica*)

The saiga (antelope) was found on the cold, arid steppes of Xinjiang where it used to graze in herds. This highly unusual ungulate has a large, flexible nose, which acts to warm the inhaled air in winter, and also as a dust-filter. Sadly, this extraordinary antelope has been hunted to extinction in China, mainly for its horns, regarded as important in TCM. However, it does still occur in some nearby countries, mainly in Kazakhstan, and it may be another candidate for reintroduction in the future.

Wild cattle

The yak (*Bos grunniens*) is a well-known shaggy-coated and very hardy close relative of cattle. Yaks are adapted to the cold of the highlands of Tibet and adjacent mountains where they graze on the generally sparse grassland. Although wild yaks can still be seen in some of the more remote spots, most are now domesticated or cross-bred with cattle, such hybrids often being referred to as dzos. Most yaks seen by tourists are fully or semi-domesticated and are herded and used in much the same manner as cattle. In the wild, adult male yaks tend to live alone while the females and calves group together. Another species of wild cattle lurks in China's southern tropical and subtropical forests, in the extreme southeast of Tibet and in southern Yunnan. This is the gaur (*B. gaurus*), a very large cow-like animal of grassland and forest. Gaur move about in small groups and are usually timid, though they can be dangerous if cornered.

Yak mother with calf. Yak often interbreed with cattle, the hybrid offspring is known as the dzo.

Gaur live in groups in warmer southern forests.

Horses

Przewalski's horse (*Equus przewalskii*), the ancestor of domestic horses, once lived wild in the northeast of Xinjiang Province, and in Inner Mongolia and Mongolia. Although it became extinct, it is now being reintroduced from captive stock. Light brown and powerfully built, it has a stiff dark brown mane. Asiatic wild ass (kiang) (*E. hemionus*) still roam on the Tibetan Plateau, where they graze in timid flocks. Although they have declined, they are still quite common in certain areas. They are chestnut brown above, with a pale or white belly and neck.

Przewalski's horses are once again roaming the steppe and semi-desert.

Asian elephant (*Elaphus maximus*)

We do not tend to associate elephants with China, but the Asian elephant can still be seen in a handful of sites. However, it occurs only in southern Yunnan, and there only in certain forested areas in Xishuangbanna, where it wanders in groups of up to several dozen. These huge animals browse on foliage and grasses in the forest and at clearings, and like to gather at ponds or riverbanks to bathe and drink. There are only a few places where elephants can still be seen, the best known is Yexianggu (Wild Elephant Valley) on the Sancha River near Mengyang, some 50km north of Jinghong.

PRIMATES

Primates are generally considered to be the most 'advanced' animals, in evolutionary terms, and comprise our closest relatives. Primates are characterised by having well-developed hands, with a separate thumb, a relatively large brain and large forward-facing eyes giving good binocular vision. As well as the higher primates (represented by monkeys and gibbons), China also has two species of lower primates in the lorises of the tropics. Monkeys and gibbons are active and inquisitive and communicate using a wide range of sounds, loud and far-carrying in the case of gibbons.

The Assamese macaque is a diurnal monkey.

Macaques

These monkeys are the most widespread and easiest to see of China's primates, and they can be quite inquisitive, especially if used to being fed by tourists. They move around in groups and spend a lot of time running or crouching on the ground, and feed on a range of food, including fruit. The rhesus macaque or rhesus monkey (*Macaca mulatta*) is the commonest of the macaques, but even this species has a scattered distribution. There are other species too, including pig-tailed macaque (*M. nemestrina*), Assamese macaque (*M. assamensis*) and stump-tailed macaque (*M. arctoides*), found in southern China, and the Tibetan macaque (*M. thibetana*). The pig-tailed macaque is a powerful monkey that just gets into China in the forests of southern Yunnan. The Tibetan macaque is endemic to China and can be observed quite easily at sites such as Emei Shan in Sichuan, where it has become accustomed to tourists.

Male Asian elephant charging with ears flapping.

A mother golden snub-nosed monkey protectively clasps her baby.

Snub-nosed monkeys

Two other groups of monkey are found in China – the snub-nosed monkeys (genus *Rhinopithecus*), and the leaf monkeys (genus *Trachypithecus*). The former have short, upturned noses and long, shaggy fur and live in certain mountain forests. The most famous is the golden snub-nosed monkey (*R. roxellana*). This rare monkey with strikingly beautiful golden fur is endemic to China, and is found in certain forests in central China, notably in Sichuan, Gansu, Shaanxi and Hubei. Even rarer is another endemic, the Yunnan snub-nosed monkey (*R. bieti*). Found in certain montane coniferous forests of northern Yunnan and southeast Tibet, they feed mainly on lichens, and also on the young leaves and shoots of trees such as birch and rowan. Only about 1,000 individuals remain in the wild, in the Yunling range in northern Yunnan and southeast Tibet, where they inhabit spruce and fir forests between about 3,500 and 4,500m. It differs from the golden snub-nosed monkey in having dark fur and a remarkable blue face. The Yunnan snub-nosed monkey has the honour of being the primate living at the highest altitude of all – up to 5,000m. A third endemic species, the Guizhou (or grey) snub-nosed monkey (*R. brelichi*) has a very limited distribution – the Fanjing Shan Nature Reserve, where only a few hundred survive.

Leaf monkeys

Leaf monkeys (also known as langurs) are more slender in build and have longer tails. François' leaf monkey (*T. francoisi*) lives in tropical monsoon forest and rocky karst hills in Guangxi, where there are only a few hundred left. White-headed leaf monkey (*T. leucocephalus*) is also restricted to southern Guangxi. Remarkably, the young of these monkeys are bright orange, while the adults are mainly black. A further species, Phayre's leaf monkey (*T. (Presbytis) phayrei*), has a scattered distribution in southwest Yunnan.

Above Golden snub-nosed monkeys live in very large social groups.
Below Phayre's leaf monkey feeds on leaves of trees.

Like other members of the group, the white-cheeked gibbon has outsized arms.

Gibbons

Perhaps the most charismatic and fascinating of China's primates are the gibbons. These long-limbed, athletic, tree-climbing apes are only found in the tropical south, especially in Yunnan. They clamber, tarzan-like, in the treetops where they like to feed on figs and other fruits, shoots, leaves and also the occasional invertebrate, and are capable of leaps of over 5m. The black gibbon (*Hylobates* [*Nomascus*] *concolor*) is found on Hainan and also in Yunnan (notably Ailao Shan and Wuliang Shan); the hoolock (white-browed) gibbon (*H.* [*Bunipithecus*] *hoolock*) in southeast Tibet and Yunnan west of the Nujiang; the white-handed (lar) gibbon (*H. lar*) only between the Nujiang and Lancangjiang; and the white-cheeked gibbon (*H. leucogenys*) is restricted to the far south of Yunnan, in Xishuangbanna. All are regarded as endangered and their numbers have been depleted through hunting (they are fairly easy to catch or shoot) and deforestation. Besides being consummate gymnasts, gibbons communicate with loud musical calls that carry long distances through the dense canopy, adding to the atmosphere of a visit to the tropical forests.

White-cheeked gibbons travel by swinging from one tree to another.

The nocturnal slow loris lives an arboreal life. (SS)

Lorises

Two more strange and mysterious primates lurk in China's tropical forests: the slow loris (*Nycticebus coucang*) and the somewhat smaller pygmy loris (*N. pygmaeus*). These are nocturnal and slow-moving with large, forward-facing eyes. They clamber about the trees using their long arms and hand-like paws, feeding mainly on fruits and insects. They are best spotted by torchlight at night, when their reflective eyes glow in the tree branches. The slow loris is found in southern Yunnan and southern Guangxi, while the pygmy loris is restricted to Yunnan.

SMALL MAMMALS

Timid and nocturnal, small mammals are generally hard to spot, although some, such as lagomorphs and many squirrels, are active by day. Hares, marmots and pikas live in open grassland, and squirrels mainly in woods and forests, while some rodents, notably jerboas and hamsters, are adapted for life in deserts. China's small mammals include a number of rare endemics, notably amongst the insectivores, lagomorphs and rodents.

Insectivores

The members of this diverse group of mammals are mostly adapted for a diet of insects and other invertebrates. Small and active, with short limbs, they have long, sensitive noses to help them locate their prey. Shrews are the main members of this group, which also contains moles and hedgehogs. The Daurian hedgehog (*Mesechinus dauuricus*) lives in the north of China, in Inner Mongolia in forests and steppe. Its close relative, the endemic Hugh's hedgehog (*M. hughi*) is found only in the north of Shaanxi and Shanxi provinces; it prefers open country, and is also found in scrub and forests.

The strange gymnures (genus *Hylomys*) are related to hedgehogs, but lack the spines. The endemic Hainan gymnure (*H. hainanensis*) is restricted to the forests of central Hainan, though the Chinese gymnure (*H. sinensis*) is more widespread in south central China. Shrews are well represented in China, with more than 40 species, several of which are endemic. The Asian house shrew (*Suncus murinus*) is sometimes found in houses in the south.

Tree shrews

Tree shrews have been variously grouped with insectivores and rodents, but they are now regarded as so distinctive that they are classified in their own order. Their appearance is most like the insectivores, but they are not closely related. One species, Berlanger's tree shrew (*Tupaia belangeri*), is found in China, in Yunnan's tropical forests. Rather like a small squirrel but with a narrow, tapering pointed snout, this tree shrew is an agile forest-dweller, feeding on insects, fruits and seeds, at home both on the forest floor and in the trees. Berlanger's tree shrew is widespread in Yunnan, but by no means that easy to spot.

Bats

Bats are flying mammals, the only vertebrates (other than birds) that are capable of powered flight. Although the bat fauna of China is not very well known (at least in the West), we do know that China has almost 100 species of bat, making it one of the richest countries in the world for this group. Two fruit bats are found in tropical southern China: the short-nosed fruit bat (*Cynopterus sphinx*) and the fulvous fruit bat (*Rousettus leschenaultii*). These large species emerge soon after sunset to feed on fruit during the night. The king horseshoe bat (*Rhinolophus rex*) is an interesting endemic with very large ears. Of special interest are the two species of bamboo bat (*Tylonycteris robustula* and *T. pachypus*), greater and lesser bamboo bats. These remarkable bats roost inside the hollow stems of bamboos, from which they emerge at dawn and dusk to feed. They fly slowly, hover frequently, and are often seen around trees and houses in villages near bamboo thickets in southern China.

Lagomorphs

This group contains rabbits, hares and pikas. Rabbits and hares are found in a wide range of habitats, from tropical forests, to open grassland, steppe and tundra, while pikas are animals of rocky mountain sites.

A number of hare species are special to China. Yunnan hare (*Lepus comus*) is found in Yunnan and also in west Guizhou. It has long, black-tipped ears and feeds

A juvenile mountain hare (*Lepus timidus*) shelters beside a rock.

in open grassland and clearings, mainly around dawn and dusk, but also during the night. The small Hainan hare (*L. hainanus*) is endemic to the dry grassland of west Hainan, while the Yarkand hare (*L. yarkandensis*) inhabits the edges of the desert in Xinjiang and the woolly hare (*L. oiostolus*) lives on the Tibetan Plateau.

Pikas are something of a China speciality too. They look like guinea pigs and live in burrows or amongst rocks in mountain and steppe habitats, remaining active throughout the winter, relying on stored grass and other food. They shun hot sunshine, although they do sometimes sunbathe if the air is very cold. They communicate by sharp piercing whistles. Chinese species include black-lipped (plateau) pika (*Ochotona curzoniae*), Helan Shan pika (*O. helanshanensis*), Koslov's pika (*O. koslowi*) and Ili pika (*O. iliensis*), the latter three endemic to China.

Pangolin (*Manis pentadactyla*)

The pangolin has to be one of the oddest of all China's wild animals. This low-slung, elongated mammal looks like an animated pine cone. It is protected by overlapping

horny plates (actually these are highly modified hairs), interspersed with normal hairs, and has sharp claws it uses for digging for ants and termites as it wanders over the forest floor, licking them up with its 20cm-long tongue. Pangolins can also swim and climb trees. They are quite widespread in Yunnan and other parts of southern China, but they have long been hunted. Their shells are used in traditional Chinese medicine, and their meat is considered a great delicacy. Pangolins spend most of the day asleep in a burrow, emerging mainly at night. When threatened, a pangolin will curl into a tight ball, face tucked under tail, and the sharp-edged scales overlapping like armour.

Rodents

Rodents are one of the most successful of all mammal groups, being found all over the world in a huge range of habitats. The order Rodentia consists of about 2,000 species, making it easily the largest of all mammalian orders. Known for their chisel-like gnawing teeth, the rodents include beavers and squirrels as well as mice, voles, gerbils, hamsters and porcupines. Most rodents are small and active, and many are nocturnal. China hosts dozens of species of

The brown rat (*Rattus norvegicus*) is an opportunist, often raiding human habitations. (AH)

mice, voles and hamsters, including many endemics. One of the more unusual mice is the pencil-tailed tree mouse (*Chiropodomys gliroides*), common in bamboo forests. Its tail has a tuft of hair at the tip – actually more like a paintbrush than a pencil! The Chinese dormouse (*Dryomys sichuanensis*) is endemic to China and lives in subalpine forests of northern Sichuan. Yet another endemic, the Chinese jumping mouse (*Eozapus setchuanus*) is a rodent of grassy woodland. It has long hind legs that allow it to make long jumps. This species and the related long-tailed birch mouse (*Sicista caudata*) can hibernate for up to six months to avoid activity in cold winter weather. The hoary bamboo rat (*Rhizomys pruinosus*) specialises in feeding on both the roots and shoots of bamboos. It has large incisor teeth and powerful neck muscles, and digs large burrow systems where it spends most of the day, emerging at night to forage in the forest. Bamboo rats can also scuttle with ease along hollow bamboo culms.

Long-tailed marmot basking on a rock.

The steppes and semi-deserts feature many small burrowing rodents such as jirds, jerboas and hamsters. Desert rodents include the endemic Cheng's jird (*Meriones chengi*) and the more widespread Mongolian jird (*M. unguiculatus*). The latter, found in northern China, is the familiar pet, usually called a gerbil. Other desert rodents include long-eared jerboa (*Euchoreutes naso*), found in the Gobi Desert and Alashan Plateau, thick-tailed pygmy jerboa (*Salpingotus crassicauda*) and five-toed pygmy jerboa (*Cardiocranius paradoxus*). Campbell's dwarf hamster (*Phodopus campbelli*), also known as Dzungarian hamster, is a popular pet. This charming hamster is native to the steppes of northern China and Russia. It is unusual in that the male assists at the birth of its offspring, cleaning the new-born young and babysitting them, and also feeding the mother. The greater long-tailed hamster (*Tscherskia triton*) is common in parts of northern China, where it can be a pest of crops.

The chunky Himalayan marmot (*Marmota himalayana*) is typical of mountain pastures, living in colonies at altitudes of up to 4,500m. The long-tailed marmot (*M. caudata*) is another common grassland species. The endemic Chinese zokor (*Myospalax fontanierii*) is an unusual rodent found in alpine meadows on the Tibetan Plateau. Zokors live almost entirely underground, feeding on roots and bulbs, creating huge burrow complexes and remaining active all through the winter, relying on caches of stored food. They only come to the surface occasionally, usually to gather seeds to take back underground.

Small and active by day, Siberian chipmunks (*Tamias sibiricus*) can often be seen, especially in the forests of the north and east. These prettily striped miniature squirrels are often found in zoos, and have also become popular as pets in recent years.

The Malayan porcupine (*Hystrix brachyura*) feeds on fallen fruits. (SS)

China also has several species of squirrel, including flying squirrels that use thin flaps of skin stretched between their outstretched limbs to glide from tree to tree. The black giant squirrel (*Ratufa bicolor*) is a large tropical species that eats mainly fruit. This impressive squirrel is active by day, running and jumping in the canopy of tropical and subtropical forests, in south Yunnan, Guangxi and Hainan. Most of the flying squirrels are tropical and nocturnal. Particoloured flying squirrel (*Hylopetes alboniger*) is found in the forests of Sichuan, Yunnan and on Hainan, while the complex-toothed flying squirrel (*Trogopterus xanthipes*) is endemic to China, and found mainly in Hunan, Guizhou, Sichuan and Yunnan. The red giant flying squirrel (*Petaurista petaurista*) feeds on fruit and nuts high in the forest canopy. It can be found in the forests of Yunnan and its gliding membrane is a bright red-brown.

The beautiful squirrels (*Callosciurus*) of the tropical forests are named for their colourful fur – patterned in black, white and orange. Chinese species include Anderson's squirrel (*Callosciurus quinquestriatus*), Pallas's squirrel (*C. erythraeus*) and Irrawaddy squirrel (*C. pygerythrus*).

Porcupines are armed with sharp, hollow quills, which are modified hairs. When threatened they rattle these and may even back into the attacker, impaling and dislodging the sharp spines. The Himalayan porcupine (*H. hodgsoni*) is fairly common in hilly grassland and woods in the south, often in cultivated areas.

WHALES, DOLPHINS AND SEALS

We do not associate China with this group of mainly marine mammals, yet China has some remarkable members. Cetaceans also occur in Chinese ocean waters, notably northern right whale (*Eubalaena glacialis*) and sperm whale (*Physeter catodon*), but we consider here just those in coastal waters and rivers.

One of the most famous was the highly unusual Yangtze river dolphin or *baiji* (*Lipotes vexillifer*). This fascinating freshwater mammal once patrolled the waters of the Yangtze and lower Fuchunjian rivers. It was a unique freshwater dolphin, endemic to China, and living exclusively in fresh water in the middle and upper reaches of the Yangtze River. The ever-increasing river traffic, combined with the technology associated with fishing, and probably also the growing pollution of the water with industrial and domestic waste, resulted in a population crash from an estimated 400 in the 1980s to 150 or even fewer in the early 1990s, making the Yangtze river dolphin one of the most critically endangered species of aquatic mammals in the world. Many attempts were made to save the species, including the establishment of special nature reserves or semi-protected sites alongside the Yangtze River, but it now looks highly doubtful that those measures have been successful. As recently as the 1950s this shy, almost blind dolphin was still quite common, but a recent survey by a team of Chinese, Swiss and American scientists failed to find any sign of its presence and has reluctantly concluded that it is almost certainly now extinct.

Amazingly, the Yangtze also hosts the world's only freshwater porpoise, the Yangtze finless porpoise (*Neophocaena phocaenoides*), although this species is also found

'Qi-Qi', a captive male Yangtze River dolphin, survived in the Wuhan dolphinarium for over 22 years. The species may now be extinct.

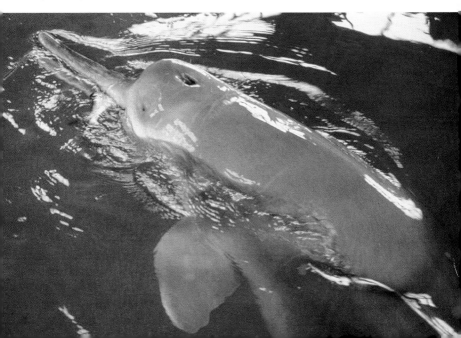

The spotted seal breeds on sea ice in the Bohai Sea.

outside China. Despite having full legal protection, it is now critically endangered here and may well follow the *baiji* into extinction. Fishing, increased river traffic and pollution have combined to reduce its population from nearly 3,000 in the late 1980s to probably well below 2,000, and it is declining at an estimated 7% a year. The good news is that the finless porpoise is being bred successfully in protected semi-natural reserves, and reintroductions into the wild may well be possible. Unfortunately, the conditions in the Yangtze River continue to decline and unless pollution can be reversed and encounters with fishing gear and boat traffic reduced, then even reintroduction may ultimately be unsuccessful.

Another dolphin is famous in China. This is the rare Chinese dolphin, a local form of the Indo-Pacific hump-backed dolphin (*Sousa chinensis*), which can still be seen in parts of Hong Kong's Pearl River estuary. The adults are a surprising pinkish colour, and these splendid creatures have become a local tourist attraction with regular dolphin-watch organised boat tours. Nevertheless, these beautiful dolphins are threatened by over-fishing, pollution and disturbance.

Another marine mammal, the dugong (*Dugong dugon*) survives in small numbers in some of China's tropical coastal waters, for example around the mangroves near the Shatian Peninsula between Guangxi and Guangdong.

Lastly, mention should be made of the spotted seal (*Phoca largha*), which breeds on the ice of the north Pacific and which may be seen at certain sites on China's northern coast, notably near Dalian.

BIRDS

The black-naped oriole feeds on berries and fruits, notable figs. (GG)

China has a large and varied bird fauna – more than 1,300 species have been recorded. We cannot include all of them here, but instead present a selection of those that are most likely to be seen, or that are otherwise prominent or especially noteworthy. Birdwatchers from Europe will find that many Chinese birds are familiar, but their birding will be considerably spiced by finding related but different species of familiar genera, as well as by quite unusual, exotic and often colourful birds from Asiatic families. Some groups are especially well represented in China – for example, the country has more cranes and pheasants than anywhere else in the world. Other groups include ducks, swans and geese, and the less familiar laughing-thrushes, parrotbills and rosefinches. Keen birdwatchers should consult a comprehensive regional bird guide (see Further Reading) for details of distribution and identification.

One of the joys of birdwatching in China, for the expert birder at least, is the chance of making a real discovery, either an extension of the range for a species within China, or perhaps even a bird new to China! Much of China is 'under-watched' and therefore the visiting birdwatcher would do well to watch carefully and be ready to expect the unexpected as well as the commoner species. To take just one example, the rare white-eared night heron (*Gorsachius magnificus*), until recently considered almost impossible to find, is now observed quite regularly in certain sites in Guangdong. Along China's southern borders in particular there are likely to be many new species added to the country's bird list in the years to come, especially in Himalayan Tibet, which is relatively unexplored and which connects with the richness of the Indian region.

SEABIRDS AND WATERBIRDS

China's wetlands and coasts are home to many birds, and some of the wetland sites are amongst the best places to watch for birds, especially for rare migrating cranes, waders and waterfowl.

Gulls and terns

These birds are graceful in flight and are usually found over sea or fresh water. Most adult gulls and terns are white, usually with black on the wingtips; the young birds are often brown or grey. Terns have narrower, pointed wings and forked tails.

The black-headed gull (*Larus ridibundus*) breeds mainly in the north, but winters further south. Pallas's (great black-headed) gull (*L. ichthyaetus*) looks like a large black-headed gull. This impressive bird breeds on certain lakes in Qinghai and Inner Mongolia, wintering mainly to the southwest. The slaty-backed gull (*L. schistisagus*) is a large gull with dark back and pink legs, which is fairly common along the coasts in winter, while the common gull (*L. canus*) breeds in the north of China and winters along the coast and at inland waters. The rare Saunders's gull (*L. saundersi*) breeds around the Yellow River delta, wintering in southeast China, notably at Mai Po. The little tern (*Sterna albifrons*) and common tern (*Sterna hirundo*) are often seen at the coast or sometimes at inland fresh water, while the whiskered tern (*Chlidonias hybridus*) breeds mainly in eastern China, and may be seen feeding at paddyfields.

Great white pelican swimming. (PS)

Pelicans and cormorants

Pelicans are very large birds with a powerful, gliding flight. They use their large, pouched bills to catch shoals of fish, sometimes by diving. They winter along the coasts and estuaries of southeast China.

The great white pelican (*Pelecanus onocrotalus*) breeds on lakes in Xinjiang and around the upper Yellow River but is not common. The somewhat larger and greyer Dalmatian pelican (*P. crispus*) is a rare breeder in northern China.

Cormorants are large, dark waterbirds that catch fish underwater using their long, hooked bills. Their feathers lack oil and get waterlogged, making them less buoyant so they can stay underwater more easily. In some parts of China tethered cormorants have been trained to catch fish and bring them back to boats, a traditional practice that has become a tourist attraction in some areas. Three species breed in China. The commonest is the great cormorant (*Phalacrocorax carbo*), which breeds on lakes (notably Qinghai Lake) and along the coast, wintering mainly in southern China.

Herons, egrets, storks and ibises

These stately, long-legged and long-necked birds are quite well represented in China, with about 20 species. Herons and egrets fly with their necks tucked in while storks fly with their necks fully extended. Herons, egrets and storks use their keen eyesight and long, dagger-like bills to catch their prey. Ibises are smaller, with curved bills, and tend to probe into the water and mud, detecting their prey mainly by touch.

There are four fairly common species of white egret. The little egret (*Egretta garzetta*) is medium-sized with black legs and yellow feet. It is regular in paddyfields and other wetlands. Less common is the much larger great egret (*Casmerodius albus*), and between these in size is the appropriately named intermediate egret (*Mesophoyx intermedia*), which occurs mainly in the south. Also quite common in the south is the small, dumpy cattle egret (*Bubulcus ibis*). The widespread grey heron (*Ardea cinerea*) is large and heavy in flight, while the slightly smaller purple heron (*A. purpurea*) is less common. The Chinese pond heron (*Ardeola bacchus*) is a small species common in rice paddies, as is the even smaller and shyer little heron (*Buturoides striatus*). At dusk in some areas the black and white, almost ghostly night heron (*Nycticorax nycticorax*) can be seen, often in paddyfields. Two small bitterns, the yellow bittern (*Ixobrychus sinensis*) and cinnamon bittern (*I. cinnamomeus*) are both quite common in reeds, swamps and paddies, but are hard to spot.

Top The great egret stands in shallow water, waiting for passing prey.
Left The oriental stork winters as far south as Hong Kong and Taiwan. (GG)

The Oriental stork (*Ciconia boyciana*) is a large white stork with a black bill. It breeds in the northeast and winters mainly in the lower Yangtze lakes. The black stork (*C. nigra*) breeds in the north and winters to marshes and other wetlands further south. Both these storks, however, are rare. The crested ibis (*Nipponia nippon*) is a fascinating bird, with a bushy crest and bright red face and legs. It is extremely rare, being found in just one colony, in Shaanxi Province, where numbers fell to just seven birds in 1981, but have since risen to about 250 under strict protection. It is also being bred in Beijing Zoo for reintroduction.

Cranes

Very much a symbol of China, and prominent in traditional art and folklore, cranes are some of China's finest birds. Most cranes are endangered, and nine of the world's 15 species are found in China. Tall and shapely, cranes are famed for their complex courtship dances, and it is this behaviour, combined with their beautiful plumage and their once mysterious migratory movements, which has given them such a central place in Chinese culture and art.

The common crane (*Grus grus*) breeds in northern China, moving to southern China in the winter. The dainty demoiselle crane (*G. virgo*) breeds in the northern

A white-naped crane bends down to drink.

The red-crowned crane shows a dazzling plumage pattern in flight.

highlands and winters in Tibet. Of greater interest to visitors from the West are five rare species of much more limited range. The red-crowned crane (*G. japonensis*) is an imposing bird, standing 1.5m tall. It is white with a red crown. It breeds in the northeast, in Heilongjiang, Liaoning and Inner Mongolia, and winters in eastern China, notably in Jiangsu Province.

The black-necked crane (*G. nigricollis*) breeds on the Tibetan Plateau and winters at lower-altitude lakes, including at some sites in Yunnan. The Siberian crane (*G. leucogeranus*) winters in large numbers to Poyang and nearby lakes. The white-naped crane (*G. vipio*) breeds in northern China and winters at lakes and rivers in the lower Yangtze basin.

Ducks, swans and geese

These waterbirds are well represented in China, several species being equally familiar in Europe. Mute swans (*Cygnus olor)* and the rarer whooper swan (*C. cygnus*) breed on lakes in the north, wintering further south, while tundra swans (*C. columbianus*) visit in winter from their Siberian breeding grounds.

Widespread and familiar geese and ducks are greylag, white-fronted and bean geese (*Anser anser, A. albifrons* and *A. fabalis*), the dabbling ducks mallard, wigeon, shoveler, pintail, garganey and common teal (*Anas platyrhynchos, A. penelope, A. clypeata, A. acuta, A. querquedula* and *A. crecca*), the diving ducks tufted duck, pochard and red-crested pochard (*Aythya fuligula, A. ferina* and *Netta rufina*) and the shelduck and ruddy shelduck (*Tadorna tadorna* and *T. ferruginea*). The sawbills – smew (*Mergus albellus*), red-breasted merganser (*M. serrator*) and goosander (*M. merganser*) – may also be spotted, or with luck the rare Chinese (scaly-sided) merganser (*M. squamatus*).

Special to China are the splendid mandarin duck (*Aix galericulata*), the male of which has wonderfully ornate plumage, falcated duck (*Anas falcata*) which resembles a green-headed wigeon, spot-billed duck (*A. poecilorhyncha*) and Baikal teal (*A. formosa*).

The last-named breeds on certain northern lakes but has become rare; the male has beautiful head and face markings. Mandarins are now rare wild, but commonly kept on lakes and parks. The lesser whistling duck (*Dendrocygna javanica*) is a tropical species that breeds in south Yunnan and south Guangxi.

More unusual species include the swan goose (*Anser cygnoides*) which breeds in the northeast and winters mainly to Poyang and Dong Ting lakes, as does the lesser white-fronted goose (*A. erythropus*), and the bar-headed goose (*A. indicus*) of highland and northern deserts and salt lakes that winters on lakes of central China. The bar-headed goose holds the bird record for high flying, having been logged at 9,150m over the Himalayas. The duck-sized cotton pygmy goose (*Nettapus coromandelianus*) is a pretty green and white species of central and southern regions.

Grebes

Grebes are compact diving waterbirds, mainly seen on open fresh water. Their feet are lobed rather then webbed, and they are expert at swimming and hunting for fish and invertebrates underwater. There are five species in China, of which the following are the commonest. The little grebe (*Tachybaptus ruficollis*) is small and dumpy and is found throughout China. The great crested grebe (*Podiceps cristatus*) is large and long-necked, with a splendid ruff in the breeding season. This, and the smaller red-necked grebe (*P. grisegena*), breed mainly in the north.

Crakes, rails and jacanas

Coot and moorhen apart, crakes and rails are mostly shy and skulking, so are hard to spot. There are about 18 species in China. They live mainly in marshy sites, such as in reedbeds, where they usually stay well out of

Top Male mandarin duck in breeding plumage.
Centre Spot-billed duck
Above Great crested grebe (M&JB)

73

sight. Many species are most active at dawn and dusk, or at night. The moorhen (*Gallinula chloropus*) is quite common in wetlands and nearby grassland, as is the more gregarious coot (*Fulica atra*) on lakes and rivers. The water rail (*Rallus aquaticus*) is also quite widespread, but is more often heard than seen (it makes pig-like squealing calls). The white-breasted waterhen (*Amaurornis phoenicurus*) can sometimes be seen in the wetlands of southern China, and brown crake (*A. akool*) breeds in swamps and rice paddies. The watercock (*Gallicrex cinerea*), large and dark and with red legs, is quite common, but mainly nocturnal. The slaty-breasted rail (*Gallirallus striatus*) lives in paddies and swamps in south China, but is hard to spot,

as are the tiny, mainly northeastern Baillon's crake *Porzana pusilla* and ruddy-breasted crake *P. fusca*, the latter both favouring reeds.

Two species of jacana occur in China. The splendid pheasant-tailed jacana (*Hydrophasianus chirurgus*) breeds through much of southern China, but it has become rare. Even rarer and restricted to Xishuangbanna is the bronze-winged jacana (*Metopidius indicus*). Jacanas are remarkable in being able to trot with ease over floating water plants, as their extremely long toes distribute their weight over a large surface area.

Waders

This group of birds is quite well represented in China, and waders are often seen wintering at coastal sites or around the margins of lakes. Several species, such as woodcock (*Scolopax rusticola*), common snipe (*Gallinago gallinago*), oystercatcher (*Haematopus ostralegus*), redshank (*Tringa totanus*), greenshank (*T. nebularia*), common sandpiper (*Actitis hypoleucos*), curlew (*Numenius arquata*), whimbrel (*Numenius phaeopus*), lapwing (*Vanellus vanellus*), dunlin (*Calidris alpina*), turnstone (*Arenaria interpres*), sanderling (*C. alba*) and godwits (*Limosa* species),

Top The white-breasted waterhen (above) is a boldly marked gallinule. (SS)
Above The elegant red-wattled lapwing (RC)

will be familiar to Western birdwatchers. Of particular note is the attractive painted snipe (*Rostratula benghalensis*), which is locally common in paddyfields and wet grassland, mainly in the south and east. The red-wattled lapwing (*V. indicus*) is most likely to be spotted in the southwest on farmland and marshes. The stately marsh sandpiper (*T. stagnatilis*) with its thin straight bill is a regular coastal passage migrant, as is the terek sandpiper (*Xenus cinereus*), whose bill is upturned. Pride of place amongst waders must go the ibisbill (*Ibidorhyncha struthersi*), surely the strangest of the group. This large black, white and grey wader has a curlew-like (but red) bill and red legs. It is a rare bird of fast rivers between 1,700 and 4,500m found in Tibet and some other central and northern mountain regions. The ibisbill has become something of a holy grail for keen birdwatchers and is the prize sighting of any mountain expedition. The swallow-like Oriental pratincole (*Glareola maldivarum*) flocks over rice paddies and marshes.

BIRDS OF PREY (RAPTORS)

Birds of prey include the huge soaring vultures, majestic eagles and smaller hawks, as well as the fish-eating osprey and several species of swift-flying falcon. They are not always easy to spot, except in the open spaces of the high mountains, plateaux or wetlands, and forest-dwelling species can often be frustratingly hidden by the canopy of trees.

Vultures, eagles and hawks

The high mountains are home to the lammergeier (*Gypaetus barbatus*) and Himalayan griffon vulture (*Gyps himalayensis*), as well as the powerful golden eagle (*Aquila chrysaetos*), while the steppe eagle (*A. nipalensis*) breeds in the steppes of the north, wintering in southern China.

A Himalayan griffon vulture soars past a mountainside.

A black-shouldered kite keeps a lookout for prey from an exposed branch. (IT)

Two small raptors of note in southern China are the black baza (*Aviceda leuphotes*) and black-shouldered kite (*Elanus caeruleus*). The former is a pied forest hawk, while the latter is a dainty kite, which has increased in recent years and may be spotted over open country. The black kite (*Milvus migrans*) and the slightly larger black-eared kite (*M. lineatus*) are commoner and can often be seen scavenging around villages. The crested goshawk (*Accipiter trivirgatus*) is widespread in hill forests of the south.

The pied harrier (*Circus melanoleucos*) is a splendid bird, the male of which has striking black and white plumage; it breeds in the northeast and winters further south. Around the southern coasts you may be lucky enough to spot the white-bellied sea eagle (*Haliaeetus leucogaster*). This large eagle soars over the sea and dives for fish.

Falcons

The kestrel (*Falco tinnunculus*), hobby (*F. subbuteo*) and peregrine (*F. peregrinus*) are all fairly widespread in China. More unusual is the dainty Amur falcon (*F. amurensis*) which breeds in the northeast. This sociable falcon is closely related to the red-footed falcon but the male has white underwing coverts. One of the smallest of all birds of prey is the tiny pied falconet (*Microhierax melanoleucos*) – a rare bird of forest edges, mainly in central and southern regions.

GROUND BIRDS

The members of the following families spend all or most of their lives on the ground, either on the forest floor, in scrub, on the open plains or on rocky plateaux.

Pheasants, partridges, grouse and quails

About 60 of the world's 200 species of the pheasant family live in China. Pheasants are mainly ground-living birds with rounded wings and often a long tail (especially the male). Males are mostly vividly coloured and patterned, while the females are a drab, camouflaged brown or grey.

China's forests are host to no fewer than 20 species, including the familiar common pheasant (*Phasianus colchicus*), which as an introduced species is now so familiar in Europe and North America, and elsewhere. Male pheasants mostly have spectacularly bright, gaudy plumage and rank amongst China's most beautiful birds.

The four species of eared-pheasant are birds of high ground. The Tibetan eared-pheasant *Crossoptilon harmani* (Tibetan Plateau) and white eared-pheasant *C. crossoptilon* (Tibetan Plateau and central China) are locally common in alpine scrub, as is the blue eared-pheasant *C. auritum* (central China). The brown eared-pheasant (*C. mantchuricum*)

Top Blue eared-pheasant showing long ear-tufts.

Above A displaying male grey peacock pheasant.

is a rare species, restricted to just a few sites in the north. The beautiful silver pheasant *Lophura nycthemera* is common in evergreen forests in southern China, while its rarer close relative the Kalij pheasant *L. leucomelanos* is a Himalayan species that gets into southeast Tibet and west Yunnan.

The golden pheasant *Chrysolophus pictus* and the related Lady Amherst's pheasant *C. amherstiae* are both familiar in the West. The former is endemic to central China where it is quite a common forest species; the latter is rarer and found mainly in the southwest. Reeves's pheasant *Syrmaticus reevesii* and Elliot's pheasant *S. ellioti* are also closely related. The male Reeves's has an extraordinarily long tail, up to 1.5m. It is a rare bird of central China's woods; known from Ba Da Gong Shan, Hunan. Elliot's is found only in southeast China, in bamboo thickets and mixed woodland. The blood pheasant *Ithaginis cruentus* is a partridge-sized bird of central China and Tibet, while the Koklass pheasant *Pucrasia macrolopha* has a wide range across central and east China but is rare. It has been recorded recently from Guan Shan, Jiangxi. The grey peacock pheasant *Polyplectron bicalcaratum* is a rare small, grey-brown species of mountain forests of Yunnan and Tibet. Even rarer is the endemic Hainan peacock pheasant *P. katsumatae*.

Monals and tragopans are chunky members of the pheasant family. They look like a cross between grouse and pheasant in build. Their typical habitat is scrub and rhododendron thickets in the mountains. Males of the satyr tragopan (*Tragopan satyra*), found in Tibet, and Temminck's tragopan (*T. temminckii*), found in Tibet and also mountains of southwest and central China, have bright red plumage. They are locally common at high altitudes.

Less common are the Chinese monal (*Lophophorus lhuysii*) and Sclater's monal

(*L. sclateri*). Monals are plump birds, the males possessing colourful and iridescent feathers in shades of purple, blue, orange and white.

As the ancestor of poultry worldwide, the red junglefowl (*Gallus gallus*) is arguably the most important member of the family. The wild form is still common in scrub and forests in southern China. The green peafowl (*Pavo muticus*) is well known from parks and bird collections in the West. However, its home is in the tropical forests of southwest China and adjacent southeast Asia, where it has entered into folklore and is the inspiration for much traditional art, as well as local ethnic minority dances. Unfortunately, generations of hunting have reduced numbers of this marvellous bird in the wild.

The large, chestnut-and-grey snow partridge (*Lerwa lerwa*) is common above the treeline in Tibet and central China where it lives in flocks. Occupying much the same habitat are the rarer Himalayan and Tibetan snowcocks (*Tetraogallus himalayensis* and *T. tibetanus*).

The chestnut-throated partridge (*Tetraophasis obscurus*), buff-throated partridge (*T. szechenyii*) and Tibetan partridge (*Perdix hodgsoniae*) are also birds of mountain rocky sites and alpine scrub, in parts of west central China and Tibet. The Daurian partridge (*P. dauuricae*) of northern China is closely related to the grey partridge of Europe. More unusual are the hill partridge (*Arborophila torqueola*) and the Chinese bamboo partridge (*Bambusicola thoracica*). The former is a local forest bird from south Tibet and west Yunnan, while the latter is endemic to central and southeast China where it inhabits bamboo groves and scrub.

The hazel grouse (*Tetrastes bonasia*) and black grouse (*Lyrurus tetrix*) will be familiar to European birders, and both species are fairly frequently seen in China's northern forests.

Small and dark with a white chin, the Chinese francolin (*Francolinus pintadeanus*) is common in scrub and forests of southern and southeast China. Buttonquails are tiny ground birds, very like quails, but are distinguished by their lack of a hind toe. Like the true quails, they are very hard to spot, and usually detected by their purring calls. The yellow-legged buttonquail (*Turnix tanki*) is fairly common across much of central and eastern China, while the barred buttonquail (*T. suscitator*) lives in south China, including Hainan.

Sandgrouse

Sandgrouse look like slim pigeons. They live in flocks in desert and steppe country, have sandy-coloured plumage and may gather in numbers to drink at pools. Two species – Pallas's sandgrouse (*Syrrhaptes paradoxus*) and Tibetan sandgrouse (*S. tibetanus*) – are locally common in the dry country of the north and west.

Bustards

These are large, long-legged and long-necked stately birds of open plains and steppes, with elaborate mating displays. Three species are known in China, of which only one, the great bustard (*Otis tarda*), is likely to be spotted, mainly on the open grasslands and semi-deserts of the north.

NEAR-PASSERINES

This is a diverse assemblage of those bird families that are midway between the generally larger birds treated above and the mostly smaller perching birds (passerines) covered in the final section.

Pigeons and doves

These are familiar fruit-and seed-eating, plump-bodied birds found mainly in wooded or mixed open country. Their calls are mainly soothing coos or croons, often rather monotonous. Some have adapted well to living close to people, especially where grain is cultivated or stored. There are about 30 species in China. In general, the larger species are called pigeons while the smaller, more delicate species are known as doves, but the distinction is not a clear one.

One of the commonest pigeons is the hill pigeon (*Columba rupestris*), which is very like the familiar rock dove/pigeon (*C. livia*) of Europe (which also gets into northwest China), but with more white in its plumage. It lives on cliffs and caves in northern mountain areas. Far more distinctive, its grey head contrasting with a white neck and breast, is the snow pigeon (*C. leuconota*), a pretty bird of alpine regions of south Tibet, north Yunnan, Sichuan and Qinghai. The speckled wood pigeon (*C. hodgsonii*), with brown-maroon plumage, is from a similar region, but lives mainly in subalpine forests.

Several medium-sized pigeons of the genus *Treron* reside in the southern tropical forests, but most are rare. The wedge-tailed green pigeon (*T. sphenura*) is local in Yunnan, Sichuan and Tibet between about 1,500 and 3,000m in heath and forests. It is colourful with bright green, orange and purple patches. Larger still are two species of imperial pigeon (genus *Ducula*),

Top The green imperial pigeon feeds up in the canopy. (ss)
Above Emerald doves seek out fallen fruit. (BB)

found in the southwest and on Hainan. The green imperial pigeon (*D. aenea*) inhabits lowland forest while the mountain imperial pigeon (*D. badia*) is found mainly in upland forests from 400 to 2,500m. Another tropical species is the ground-dwelling emerald dove (*Chalcophaps indica*), which has bright, shiny emerald green wings.

The commonest doves of the turtle dove genus *Streptopelia* are the Oriental turtle dove (*S. orientalis*), which is very like the European turtle dove, and spotted dove (*S. chinensis*), which has a black patch, spotted with white, on its neck. Both are quite common over most of the country and also around villages and fields, as is the familiar collared dove (*S. decaocto*). The dainty red-collared dove (*S. tranquebarica*) is a bird of dry forest and open woodland. It is small and pink, with a grey-blue head.

A female rose-ringed parakeet flying into nesting hole. (CN)

Parrots

Parrots and parakeets are lively, noisy, intelligent birds, mainly found in tropical forests. Eight species occur in China. They are fast-flying, fruit-eating birds with powerful beaks and colourful plumage. Two native species are not uncommon in their relatively restricted ranges and both are mainly green, with blue-grey head and long tail. The grey-headed parakeet (*Psittacula finschiii*) and the larger derbyan parakeet (*P. derbiana*) live in subtropical forests in Yunnan, southwest Sichuan and southeast Tibet, the latter in montane forests to 4,000m. The red-breasted parakeet (*P. alexandri*) is rarer, and is found mainly in Hainan, Guangxi and Yunnan. A few other species have been introduced and become established, mainly in Hong Kong, including the yellow-crested cockatoo (*Cacatua sulphurea*), rainbow lorikeet (*Trichoglossus haematodus*) and the cosmopolitan rose-ringed parakeet (*Psittacula krameri*).

Cuckoos and coucals

Cuckoos are fast-flying birds with long wings and long tails. They feed mainly on insects and many are well known as brood parasites, laying their eggs in the nests of unrelated 'host' species. Some have hawk-like barred and streaked plumage, and many cuckoos have characteristic, monotonous calls. There are 16 Chinese species. The common cuckoo (*Cuculus canorus*) is a summer visitor to most of China and, as in Europe favours woodland and also reedbeds. Rather similar are the shy Oriental cuckoo (*C. saturatus*), which prefers higher ground, and the Indian cuckoo (*C. micropterus*) of lowland forests. These three cuckoos are best distinguished by their calls.

The female Asian koel lays eggs in other species' nests. (GG)

The large hawk cuckoo (*Hierococcyx sparverioides*) breeds in forests from Tibet across central and southern China, and the smaller Hodgson's hawk cuckoo (*H. fugax*) has a range extending to the far northeast. The hawk cuckoos have penetrating repetitive calls. The Asian koel (*Eudynamys scolopacea*) is easily recognised by its repeated loud calls that it utters with irritating persistence, even during the night. The male is black and the female barred grey-brown – both have striking red eyes. The green-billed malkoha (*Phaenicophaeus tristis*) is a grey, long-tailed cuckoo from the tropical south and has a frog-like call. It is fairly common in south Guangxi. Also southern is the small plaintive cuckoo (*Cacomantis merulinus*), which though common is quite hard to spot (as are many cuckoos).

Coucals are related to cuckoos, but are not parasitic. There are two species in China, both with dark bodies and chestnut wings. The greater coucal (*Centropus sinensis*) is common in the southern lowlands, from forests to reeds and mangroves, while the lesser coucal (*C. bengalensis*) prefers scrub and grassland.

Owls, nightjars and relatives

Owls are mainly nocturnal hunters. They have large eyes and most have dark plumage. Many species make strange hooting or shrieking calls. There are about 30 species in China, but most are either rare or of restricted range, or both. Both the tawny owl (*Strix aluco*) and long-eared owl (*Asio otus*) are common over most of the country, the former in temperate woodland, the latter breeding mainly in northern coniferous woods. The little owl (*Athene noctua*) is also common, mainly in the north and west. Even smaller are the Asian barred owlet (*Glaucidium cuculoides*) and collared owlet (*G. brodiei*), both of which are fairly common. The collared owlet is one of the world's smallest owls at only 16cm, yet even so it is an able hunter of small birds and is regularly mobbed by them. Also small are the scops owls, which have beautifully cryptic plumage and neat ear-tufts. The Oriental scops owl (*Otus sunia*) is quite common, as is the rather larger collared scops owl (*O. bakkamoena*).

The best way to locate and identify owls, especially the scops owls, is by learning their distinctive calls. The four-note call of the collared owlet is a common sound in the woods of central and southern China.

At the other end of the owl scale are the eagle owls. The Eurasian eagle owl (*Bubo bubo*) is a magnificent bird and found scattered over most of China, though not easy

The spotted owlet (*Athene brama*) replaces the little owl in China's far south-west. (SS)

to see. This huge owl, reaching 70cm and with a wingspan of 2m, likes forests with cliffs, mountains and quarries.

Nightjars are strange, mainly nocturnal, insect-eating birds that have long wings and highly cryptic plumage. There are about five species in China. The European nightjar (*Caprimulgus europaeus*) is a rare species, found only in the far north (mainly Altai and Tian Shan), but the grey nightjar (*C. indicus*) is much more widespread, in mountain forest and scrub. In the tropical south the large-tailed nightjar (*C. macrurus*) and savannah nightjar (*C. affinis*) are locally common. The former is also found in mangroves, while the latter sometimes nests on tall buildings in cities. Hodgson's frogmouth (*Batrachostomus hodgsoni*) is related to nightjars. It is a rare bird of forest in southeast Tibet and southwest Yunnan.

A large-tailed nightjar at its daytime roost. (SS)

Swifts

Swifts are well named. Their narrow wings and rapid wingbeats propel them through the skies at great speed. Nine species occur in China. The common swift (*Apus apus*) is common in the north, while the smaller house (little) swift (*A. affinis*), which has a white throat and rump, is common in the south. The fork-tailed swift (*A. pacificus*) is also common over much of China. The white-throated needletail (*Hirundapus caudacutus*) is a large swift found on the Tibetan Plateau and nearby mountain regions and also in the far northeast. Strongly associated with fan-palm trees, the charming Asian palm swift (*Cypsiurus balasiensis*) is locally common in Yunnan and Hainan. Finally, the Himalayan swiftlet (*Aerodramus (Collocalia) brevirostris*) breeds in rock crevices and caves in parts of Tibet, Sichuan and Yunnan, notably at the so-called 'Swallow's Cavern' near Jianshui, Yunnan, where the nests are collected to make bird's nest soup. The true edible-nest swiftlet is *A. (C.) fuciphaga*, which does not breed in China. China's most unusual swift is the remarkable crested treeswift (*Hemiprocne coronata*), a rare bird of the forests of southwest Yunnan. It is quite unmistakable, mainly grey with long narrow wings and tail and a crest at the base of the bill, and the males have bright orange cheeks.

Kingfishers, rollers, bee-eaters and hoopoes

Kingfishers are exciting birds – with their lively behaviour and bright colours they have great appeal. There are nine species in China, most of which feed mainly by diving into water for fish, amphibians and invertebrate larvae, which they catch in their dagger-like bills. The familiar common kingfisher (*Alcedo atthis*) has a wide distribution in Europe and Asia, including most of China. Similar, but somewhat darker blue is the rare blue-eared kingfisher (*A. meninting*) of Xishuangbanna's forest streams. Blyth's kingfisher (*A. hercules*) is like a larger version of the common kingfisher; it is a rare resident in south and southeast China, including southeast Tibet, south Yunnan and Hainan, on large forest streams.

The white-throated (*Halcyon smyrnensis*) and black-capped kingfishers (*H. pileata*) are closely related, with heavy red bills and blue-and-white plumage, the former

with a brown cap, the latter black. The former is mainly a southern species found on varied wetlands, while the latter has a wider range and is mainly a river bird. The pied kingfisher (*Ceryle rudis*) is a black and white bird often hovering before a dive over ponds and lakes. Largest of all is the crested kingfisher (*Megaceryle lugubris*), which is also mainly black and white. It favours rocky rivers. Smallest of all is the cute Oriental dwarf kingfisher (*Ceyx erithacus*), a rare bird of tropical streams, found mainly in Yunnan, Hainan and Guangxi.

The Oriental dwarf kingfisher is confined to forests. (SS)

The pied kingfisher scans for prey while hovering. (IT)

Rollers are crow-sized birds of open mixed country. They are brightly coloured with long wings. Two species are commonly found in China – the Indian roller (*Coracias benghalensis*) and the dollarbird (*Eurystomus orientalis*). The former has a complex pattern of blues, greys and pinks, with bright blue patches on the wings and tail, while the latter is a dark blue-grey bird with pale blue wing patches and a vivid, deep red bill.

Bee-eaters are streamlined, active hunters of bees and other flying insects. They have bright, often iridescent plumage, and are graceful, buoyant and very acrobatic in flight. Six species occur in China, mainly in the south. Commonest is the blue-tailed bee-eater (*Merops philippinus*), which is mainly green with a yellow throat and bright blue tail. The smaller chestnut-headed bee-eater (*M. leschenaulti*) is fairly common in southeast Tibet and west Yunnan.

The hoopoe (*Upupa epops*) has no close relatives and is very distinctive (*see p86*), with peachy body plumage, broad wings banded in black and white, a down-curved bill, a long crest and butterfly-like floppy flight. Hoopoes are found over most of China, in the lowlands and hill country.

A hoopoe carrying food for its nestlings. (SH)

Woodpeckers, barbets, trogons and hornbills

Woodpeckers are superbly adapted to climbing and feeding in trees. They have stiff tails to steady themselves against a trunk or branch, and chisel-like bills for hammering and probing into the wood for grubs and for excavating nest-holes. Their flight is deeply undulating. China has about 30 species of woodpecker. Both great spotted (*Dendrocopos major*) and lesser spotted (*D. minor*) woodpeckers are locally common, the former throughout most of China, the latter mainly in the northeast. Also mainly in the northeast is the white-backed woodpecker (*D. leucotos*), though this species is also found in certain mountains in central and eastern China (notably Wuyishan and the Qinling range). The three-toed woodpecker (*Picoides tridactylus*) has a comparable disjunct distribution – the far northeast and southeast Tibet and bordering Yunnan and Sichuan. The all red-brown rufous woodpecker (*Celeus brachyurus*) is occasional in open forest in the south.

There are about half a dozen species of 'green' woodpecker (genus *Picus*), of which the grey-headed (*P. canus*) is the most widespread, the other species being either of restricted range or rare. The black woodpecker (*Dryocopus martius*) is jet black and large, but uncommon in forests from central to northeast China. Its close relative the white-bellied woodpecker (*D. javensis*) is a bird of lowland forests in Yunnan and Sichuan, but again is not very common. Most striking are the flamebacks, which are medium-sized and brightly coloured, with red head and rump and black and white undersides; they are birds of the tropical southwest. The common flameback (*Dinopium javanense*) and greater flameback (*Chrysocalaptes lucidus*) are local, mainly in Xishuangbanna.

The strange, grey-brown wryneck (*Jynx torquilla*) is widespread and can often be located by its nasal call. Widespread, but not that common, is the grey-capped pygmy woodpecker (*D. canicapillus*), which is as small as the lesser spotted. Largest of all, at 50cm, is the great slaty woodpecker (*Mulleripicus pulverulentus*). Almost entirely grey, this magnificent bird is a real find in the lowland forests of south Yunnan and southeast Tibet. Mention should also be made of the tiny, charming piculets, dumpy woodland birds resembling tits in both size and behaviour, favouring forests and bamboo groves. The speckled piculet (*Picumnus innominatus*) is quite widespread in central and southern China, while the even smaller white-browed piculet (*Sasia ochracea*) is restricted to the far southwest.

The female common flameback has a black and white crown. (SS)

The great hornbill has an outrageously outsized bill. (SS)

Barbets are colourful fruit-eating woodland birds with large bills. China has eight species, mainly in southern forests. They are colourful with long tails, and short, stout bills specialised for feeding on insects. The great barbet (*Megalaima virens*) is fairly common in the forests of southern China to about 2,000m. The blue-throated barbet (*M. asiatica*) is only found in the southwest, mainly in south Yunnan. Trogons (three species in China, all uncommon) are tropical. The red-headed trogon (*Harpactes erythrocephalus*) inhabits tropical and subtropical forests scattered across southern China, including Hainan.

Hornbills are large tree-nesting birds with long, heavy bills. There are five species in China, all found in southern tropical forests, and all rare. Largest, at 125cm, is the great hornbill (*Buceros bicornis*), a magnificent mainly black and white bird of lowland forests in southeast Tibet and southwest Yunnan. The Oriental pied hornbill (*Anthracoceros albirostris*), found in open forest in the same region and in south Guangxi, is also mainly black and white, but much smaller at about 75cm.

PASSERINES (PERCHING BIRDS)

Perching birds (passerines) are by far the largest group of birds, accounting for about 60% of all bird species. This group contains many varied families, from large crows to tiny wrens and leaf-warblers, and many have complex and attractive songs. Identifying songbirds can be a challenging business, especially in the subtropical and tropical forests where birds flit rapidly into the undergrowth and where there can also be flocks containing several species. Local expert advice is essential, as is a good knowledge of calls and songs. Here we can offer no more than a taster to some of the larger and more difficult groups.

Pittas, fairy bluebirds and leafbirds

Pittas are attractive and colourful birds of the forest floor. There are eight species in China, but nearly all of them are rare and restricted to tropical forests in the south. The fairy pitta (*Pitta nympha*), however, is more widespread, breeding across eastern China and as far north as Korea and Japan.

Fairy bluebirds (one species in China) and leafbirds (three species in China) are an eastern family of green woodland and forest birds. The Asian fairy bluebird (*Irena puella*) is a common lowland forest bird in southern Yunnan. The male of this beautiful species is impressive – bright blue above, mainly black beneath; the female is green. The commonest of the group is the orange-bellied leafbird (*Chloropsis hardwickii*), found in forests in southern China, including Hainan. It is green above with an orange belly, and the male has a bright blue throat and wingpatch. Leafbirds have sweet, musical songs and calls.

Shrikes

Like miniature hawks, shrikes are predatory perching birds with sharply hooked beaks. They eat mostly large insects and small vertebrates. About ten species are found in China. They favour thorny scrub and semi-deserts. The long-tailed shrike (*Lanius schach*) is common over much of central and south China and the grey-backed shrike (*L. tephronotus*) is found mainly in the west, and at higher altitudes. The brown shrike (*L. cristatus*) and tiger shrike (*L. tigrinus*) range from central to northeast China.

Crows and relatives

The crow family is very large, consisting of crows and their various relatives (30 species in China), as well as related groups such as orioles (six species), minivets (eight species), woodswallows (one species), cuckooshrikes (two species), fantails (three species), paradise flycatchers (three species), ioras (two species) and drongos (seven species).

The Eurasian jay (*Garrulus glandarius*) and magpie (*Pica pica*) will be familiar to visitors from Europe, and both are found through most of China. Also of Eurasian distribution are the nutcracker (*Nucifraga caryocatactes*), red- and yellow-billed choughs (*Pyrrhocorax pyrrhocorax* and *P. graculus*), rook (*Corvus frugilegus*), carrion crow

The large-billed crow is common over much of China.

(*C. corone*) and raven (*C. corax*). The nutcracker is a bird of subalpine and northern conifer forests, the chough and raven occur on high-altitude plateaux and mountains, mainly western, while the rook and carrion crow are mainly northern. Two other common large crows are the large-billed crow (*C. macrorhynchos*) and the collared crow (*C. torquatus*), the latter glossy and black and white.

The common jackdaw of China is the Daurian jackdaw (*C. dauuricus*), a very smart bird with white belly and neck. The azure-winged magpie (*C. cyana*) is a splendid bird, common in parks and gardens, mainly in east and northeast China, but also scattered elsewhere. Another striking crow is the red-billed blue magpie (*Urocissa erythrorhyncha*), a beautiful blue bird with a long tail that lives in noisy flocks. Less easy to see is the green magpie (*Cissa chinensis*), a shy bird of the southwest subtropical forests. The sandy-coloured Mongolian and Xinjiang ground jays (*Podoces hendersoni* and *P. biddulphi*) are interesting birds of the northwestern deserts and steppe.

Rufous treepies frequent the crowns of small trees. (SS)

Mention should also be made of the treepies. The grey treepie (*Dendrocitta formosae*) and rufous treepie (*D. vagabunda*) are russet and grey, with long tails, the former found in the south and central China, the latter only in the southwest. The drongo-like ratchet-tailed treepie (*Temnurus temnurus*) is small and black; its forked tail has saw-like edges. It is a rare bird of Hainan and Guangxi.

Orioles are smart, often colourful birds with melodious calls. The golden oriole (*Oriolus oriolus*) gets into northwest China, typically in poplar stands, while the black-naped oriole (*O. xanthornus*) is much more widespread in central and eastern areas. The maroon oriole (*O. traillii*) is an uncommon bird of the southwest and Hainan, and the silver oriole (*O. mellianus*) is a rare species found locally from south Sichuan to Guangdong.

Large and black-winged cuckooshrikes (*Coracina macei* and *C. melaschistos*) are locally common birds of open woodland, mainly in the south. Smaller and more colourful (males red and black; females yellow and black) are the minivets (*Pericrocotus*). The long-tailed minivet (*P. ethologus*) is fairly common in central and southwest China, while the rosy minivet (*P. roseus*), short-billed minivet (*P. brevirostris*) and scarlet minivet (*P. flammeus*) are southern species.

Bold and noisy with striking forked tails, drongos are usually quite easy to spot. Black, ashy and spangled drongos (*Dicrurus macrocercus*, *D. leucophaeus* and *D. hottentottus*)

The male short-billed minivet has striking plumage.

are quite widespread, while the magnificent greater racket-tailed drongo (*D. paradiseus*), with its long, wire-like outer tail feathers, is a noisy bird of the forests in the deep southwest.

The Asian paradise flycatcher (*Terpsiphone paradisi*) must be one of China's most beautiful woodland birds, and is quite common over much of the country, except the far north and northwest. The male has long, curving central tail feathers and is either mainly chestnut, or pure white; the head of both forms being black. The black-naped monarch (*Hypothymis azurea*) is a very pretty southern monarch-flycatcher, with bright blue plumage.

THE AZURE-WINGED MAGPIE PUZZLE

The azure-winged magpie (*Cyanopica cyanus*) is a beautiful member of the crow family, and a great favourite with birdwatchers. It is a rather tame, noisy and sociable bird and this behaviour, combined with the attractive plumage, makes it easy to spot wherever it occurs.

European birders know this species from central Spain and Portugal where a local population is established. The strangest thing about this species is that it is also found in the Far East, in China, 9,000km from its localities in Iberia. The eastern range includes much of China, Korea, Japan, northern Mongolia and southeast Russia. The Asian birds are slightly larger, with a longer tail and paler plumage, but otherwise they are very similar to those in Iberia.

Two serious explanations have been proposed for this strange situation. One is that travellers, possibly Marco Polo or Portuguese sailors, brought the birds back from their Oriental expeditions and introduced them to Spain. The other is that the birds' range was once more extensive and continuous across the whole of Asia, but glaciations interrupted the central link, leaving the two populations far apart. Yet neither of these theories seems very satisfactory.

Recently, bones probably belonging to this species were found in a cave in Gibraltar and dated at over 44,000 years, thus indicating that the bird is indeed native to Iberia and not introduced. Modern genetics has also now come to the aid of ornithologists and shown that the European population is sufficiently distinct genetically from the Asian, and that they are indeed native to Iberia. It has been suggested that the Iberian birds be given full species status, as *Cyanopica cooki*, a name originally given to a Spanish specimen in 1850.

A white-throated dipper carries a beakful of aquatic insects. (DMc)

Dippers

Plump waterbirds, dippers are at home on clear mountain streams where they dive and walk underwater to catch insect larvae and the like. There are two species in China. The white-throated dipper (*Cinclus cinclus*), familiar from Europe, is fairly common in the highlands of the west, while the all-dark brown dipper (*C. pallasii*) has a wider distribution over much of China.

Thrushes, chats and true flycatchers

This is a large family containing several familiar species, many of which have musical songs. Most are ground-feeders, taking a wide range of invertebrate prey, though flycatchers feed mostly by swooping after flying insects. There are more than 120 species in China, including thrushes, robins, chats, flycatchers and relatives.

Familiar Eurasian species also found in China are the Eurasian blackbird (*Turdus merula*), blue rock thrush (*Monticola solitarius*), bluethroat (*Luscinia svecica*), black redstart (*Phoenicurus ochruros*) and stonechat (*Saxicola torquata*). Less familiar to Western visitors is the scaly (White's) thrush (*Zoothera dauma*), a large mottled thrush of forests, with black and white stripes on the underwing. Its relative, the

orange-headed thrush (*Z. citrina*), is a common woodland bird. Another is the black-breasted thrush (*T. dissimilis*) found in the hills of the southwest. This is a dainty thrush with black head and breast (male) and orange flanks. The chestnut thrush (*T. rubrocanus*) is chestnut with a grey head and is found mainly in subalpine forests in the highlands of the southwest.

The lesser and white-browed shortwings (*Brachypteryx leucophrys* and *B. montana*) are stumpy robin-like birds of montane forests in central and southern regions; the males are slaty-grey. The Oriental magpie robin (*Copsychus saularis*) is common in woods, parks and gardens in southern China, and

The striking male orange-headed thrush. (ss)

can be quite tame. Hodgson's and Daurian redstarts (*Phoenicurus hodgsoni* and *P. auroreus*) are locally common colourful redstarts of subalpine forests, and the white-capped water redstart (*Chaimarrornis leucocephalus*) is a delightful bird of mountain rivers and streams, often seen on mid-stream boulders.

Another charming bird of mountain streams and waterfalls is the black and white little forktail (*Enicurus scouleri*). There are four other forktails, all found along streams, and all black and white with long tails, one of the most widespread being the white-crowned forktail (*E. leschenaulti*). Northern, pied, desert and isabelline wheatears (*Oenanthe oenanthe, O. pleschanka, O. deserti* and *O. isabellina*) may all be seen in the deserts and steppes of the north.

Flycatchers are well represented in China's woods and forests, but they can be hard to identify. The rufous-gorgeted flycatcher (*Ficedula strophiata*), small and dainty with a red throat patch, is a common though shy bird of the southwest and Tibet. One of the prettiest of all is the fairly common yellow-rumped flycatcher (*F. zanthopygia*), which is black and white with a yellow rump and underparts. The Mugimaki flycatcher (*F. mugimaki*) has a robin-like red breast and is found mainly in the forests of the far northeast.

Niltavas are flycatchers, found mainly in the southwest. The males have mostly blue plumage. The small and Fujian niltavas (*Niltava macgrigoriae* and *N. davidi*) are fairly common in forests. The male of the former is almost entirely blue, while males of the latter are blue with an orange belly. The grey-headed canary flycatcher (*Culicicapa ceylonensis*) is green, with a grey head and yellow belly. This pretty flycatcher is also quite common in the forests of the southwest.

Starlings and mynas

These are medium-sized, generally noisy and sociable birds, many known for their mimicry and whistling calls. They feed predominantly on fruit and invertebrates and mostly nest in holes in trees. Several are popular as cage birds, partly because they can be taught tunes and voices. There are 19 species in China. The red-billed starling (*Sturnus sericeus*) is quite common over much of central and southeast China; it is grey and white with a red bill. The white-shouldered starling (*S. sinensis*), which is also mainly grey but with white shoulder patches, is a southern species, largely replaced further north by the darker grey white-cheeked starling (*S. cineraceus*). Mainly tropical in the far south is the larger black-collared starling (*S. nigricollis*). In the southwest, the common mynah (*Acridotheres tristis*) is quite common around fields and villages, while the commonest mynah of most of central and southern China is the crested mynah (*A. cristatellus*). The most famous, due to its popularity as a cage bird, is the hill mynah (*Gracula religiosa*), found in the tropical southwest.

Nuthatches and wallcreepers

China is something of a hotspot for nuthatches, with no fewer than 11 species of these woodland birds occurring, though most of these are uncommon or rare. The wallcreeper (*Tichodroma muraria*) is a strange bird of cliffs and mountains. It is not uncommon in mountain regions and can even be seen scaling the sides of tall buildings of nearby towns in the winter – I well remember one ascending the cliff-like wall of a modern hotel in Lijiang, in north Yunnan. The Eurasian nuthatch (*Sitta europaea*) is quite common in central and eastern China. The Yunnan nuthatch (*S. yunnanensis*) is a pale species found in upland pine forests of Yunnan, Sichuan and nearby regions. The giant nuthatch (*S. magna*) is larger and darker and found in similar sites, while the velvet-fronted nuthatch (*S. frontalis*), also of the southwest, is a charming bird with a blue back and bright red bill.

Treecreepers and wrens

China has four species of treecreeper. These small, cryptically coloured birds creep mouse-like, generally in spirals, up the trunks of trees and can be quite hard to spot. The Eurasian treecreeper (*Certhia familiaris*) is fairly common in the forests of the north, while the other species are mainly Himalayan and get into southwest China. The rusty-flanked treecreeper (*C. nipalensis*) is common in coniferous woods in southeast Tibet and west Yunnan (notably Gaoligongshan). The common (winter) wren (*Troglodytes troglodytes*) is widespread across much of China.

Tits and long-tailed tits

Of the 27 species in China, coal, great, marsh, willow and long-tailed tits (*Parus ater, P. major, P. palustris, P. montana* and *Aegithalos caudatus*) are all fairly common, especially in the north and east. In the southeast the coal tit is replaced by the similar yellow-bellied tit (*Pardaliparus venustulus*); it is very like a coal tit, but with a bright yellow belly. In central and western China, the green-backed tit (*Parus monticolus*) is like a great tit, but is more boldly marked, and green above. Also large, and highly distinctive, is the yellow-cheeked tit (*Parus spilonotus*), a southern species with bright yellow and green plumage and a crest. The pretty blue azure tit (*Parus cyanus*) is found in the far northeast and northwest, while the black-throated tit (*Aegithalos concinnus*), related to the long-tailed tit but with a shorter tail and orange cap, is common in central and southern regions. China's most striking tit is the sultan tit (*Melanochlora sultanea*). Large, yellow and black, with a yellow crest, this splendid species is a bird of lowland evergreen forests in the tropical south, including Hainan.

Swallows and martins

China has 13 species of these elegant aerial insect-eaters. The sand martin (*Riparia riparia*), barn swallow (*Hirundo rustica*) and red-rumped swallow (*H. daurica*) are all widespread, with the first being replaced by the similar plain martin (*R. paludicola*) in the far southwest. The house martin (*Delichon urbica*) builds its mud nests mainly in the far north and is replaced in the south and central regions by the Asian house martin (*D. dasypus*),

Top The yellow-cheeked tit has a pronounced crest.
Above House martin collecting mud for its nest. (DH)

which has dark patches under the wings. The striated swallow (*H. striolata*) looks like a more heavily streaked red-rumped swallow, and is found in south and west Yunnan.

Left The black bulbul eats fruit and insects.
Right The crested finchbill sports an upturned crest above an ivory-coloured bill.

Bulbuls and finchbills

These jaunty birds with liquid, musical calls number some 20 species in China. Among the commoner bulbuls are the red-whiskered and black-crested (*Pycnonotus jocosus* and *P. melanicterus*) in the south and southwest, and the mainly southeastern light-vented bulbul (*P. sinensis*). The sooty-headed bulbul (*P. aurigaster*) is also fairly common in the south, while the black bulbul (*Hypsipetes leucocephalus*) is common in southern evergreen hill forests. The collared finchbill (*Spizixos semitorques*) is green with a heavy bill, and is found in southeast China. The crested finchbill is another attractive and widespread species, which forms large pre-roost gatherings.

Prinias and cisticolas

These warbler-like birds are mostly dull-coloured, active and noisy, though rather shy, and most are found in scrub and reeds. Cisticolas are small and compact, while most prinias are somewhat larger and have long, graduated tails.

Warblers, white-eyes and relatives

A large group with about 95 species, some very similar – this is another group for the specialist. The rufous-faced warbler (*Abroscopus albogularis*) is prettily marked, with reddish cheeks, a green back and yellow rump and chest. It is fairly common in southern bamboo thickets and forest. One unusual warbler relative is the common tailorbird (*Orthotomus sutorius*), found in the south, in open forests and gardens. Green-backed and chestnut-capped, it has a long, cocked tail, and a persistent call. It is famous for creating its nest from two leaves stitched together with grass.

The island of Hainan has its very own endemic warbler, the Hainan leaf warbler (*Phylloscopus hainanus*), which is green-backed and bright yellow beneath. White-eyes

(*Zosterops*) are small greenish warbler-like birds with an obvious white ring around the eye. There are three species in China: the Japanese white-eye (*Z. japonicus*) is central and southern; the chestnut-flanked white-eye (*Z. erythropleurus*) breeds in the northeast; while the Oriental white-eye (*Z. palpebrosus*) is southwestern.

Babblers, fulvettas and relatives

This is a large and varied, mainly southern group containing about 80 species in China, and including the warbler-like fulvettas and yuhinas. Most of these birds will be unfamiliar to the Western tourist, but they tend to be rather obvious, with loud songs and raucous calls. Even expert ornithologists find many of these songbirds a challenge, so again we will mention just a small selection. The spot-breasted scimitar-babbler (*Pomatorhinus erythrocnemis*), brown with a curved bill, is common in scrub across central and eastern China. The rufous-capped babbler (*Stachyris ruficeps*), grey, with chestnut cap, is a small tree babbler of scrub and bamboo. The red-billed leiothrix (*Leiothrix lutea*) will be familiar to anyone interested in cage birds, as it is commonly kept as a pet (and often described as 'Pekin robin' in aviculture). The related silver-eared mesia (*L. argentauris*) is a dazzling babbler of southwest China. Brown and streaked, the Chinese babax (*Babax lanceolatus*) is a noisy ground-feeding babbler.

Top A Japanese white-eye feeding on *Erythrina* flowers. (GG)
Above The red-billed leiothrix moves in noisy flocks. (GG)

Fulvettas (*Alcippe*) are warbler-like babbler relatives that typically flit about in flocks in the undergrowth, constantly on the move. The grey-cheeked fulvetta (*A. morrisonia*) looks similar to a common whitethroat – brownish, with a blue-grey head. Yuhinas (*Yuhina*) are also rather warbler-like in appearance (although they have crests), and noisy and flocking in behaviour. The striated and black-chinned yuhinas (*Y. castaniceps* and *Y. nigrimenta*) are both common in the montane forests of central and southern areas, as is the attractive white-collared yuhina (*Y. diademata*) in the central highlands.

Laughingthrushes and liocichlas

This group is another of China's ornithological specialities, the country having 37 of the world's total of 53 species. The name comes from their thrush-like appearance and behaviour, and their raucous, often laughing calls. Many species also have musical songs. They tend to move about in flocks, maintaining contact through repeated calls. They are commonly trapped and kept as cage birds, and may be seen in public parks, where the cages are hung close to each other and the birds

Top Emei Shan liocichla (GG)
Centre Eurasian skylark (DH)
Above Male horned lark (DMc)

stimulated into a competitive chorus of song. Here we can only mention a few of the more prominent or common species. The masked laughingthrush (*Garrulax perspicillatus*), grey-brown with a dark mask, is a common bird of lowland of central and southern areas, and is also seen in parks. The black-throated laughingthrush (*G. chinensis*) is common in lowland forests and scrub in the far south. The hwamei (*G. canorus*) is a common small, brown laughingthrush of central and southern China. It is often trapped and caged for its tuneful song. The Emei Shan liocichla (*Liocichla omeiensis*) has the distinction of having a very limited distribution – the holy mountain of Emei Shan in Sichuan and some other nearby ranges. It is a pretty bird, olive-grey with bright orange wingbars and a red-tipped tail.

Parrotbills

Our only parrotbill in Europe is the bearded tit (*Panurus biarmicus*), a species also found in reedbeds in northern China. Although this species has a rather small bill, the other parrotbills live up to their name and have deep bills, notched like those of parrots. Two of the commoner species are the grey-headed parrotbill (*Paradoxornis gularis*) and the spot-breasted parrotbill (*P. guttaticollis*), found in scrub and bamboo in central and southern regions. Another common species is the much smaller vinous-throated parrotbill (*P. webbianus*), which tends to move around in flocks. The reed parrotbill (*P. heudei*) looks similar to the bearded tit, but has the parrot-like bill. It is found only in the far northeast, in the lower Yangtze area, and notably, at Dafengmilu NR in Jiangsu Province.

Larks, pipits and wagtails

The Eurasian skylark (*Alauda arvensis*) is quite common over northern China. The larger Tibetan lark (*Melanocorypha maxima*), reddish with a heavy bill, is found on the Tibetan Plateau, while the pretty horned lark (*Eremophila alpestris*) occurs in the same region, and also further north into the deserts and steppes. Noteworthy amongst pipits is the large, long-legged Richard's pipit (*Anthus richardi*), common in summer over much of the country, in open grassy sites. All three familiar European wagtails – white, yellow and grey (*Motacilla alba, M. flava* and *M. cinerea*) – are common, as is the pretty citrine wagtail (*M. citreola*), with pure yellow breast and head, the latter mainly in the north and west. The forest wagtail (*Dendronanthus indicus*) is a charming, tame species of the forest floor. It has a striking double black breast-band, and is found mainly in central and northeast China.

Sunbirds and flowerpeckers

These are mostly colourful birds, mainly found in the tropical south and southwest. Sunbirds are the hummingbirds of the Old World, with fine long bills, and can hover and sip nectar from flowers, though some also take pollen and insects. Flowerpeckers have larger, shorter bills and feed mainly on insects and berries. One of the commoner sunbirds is Mrs Gould's sunbird (*Aethopyga gouldiae*), which often feeds on rhododendron flowers in montane forests. The male is orange, with a blue chin, yellow rump and a long blue tail; the female is mainly green. Also common is the fork-tailed sunbird (*A. christinae*), a southeastern lowland species that sometimes feeds in gardens, as is the crimson sunbird (*A. siparaja*) in the southwest. The plain flowerpecker (*Dicaeum concolor*) lives up to its name, being a dull grey-green; it is common in southern China. Also

Male Mrs Gould's sunbird.

common is the more colourful fire-breasted flowerpecker (*D. ignipectus*); the male is greenish-blue above, pale below, with a red throat patch. The yellow-vented flowerpecker (*D. chrysorrheum*) is common in parts of southern Yunnan; the male is grey-green above, with yellow under the tail and a streaked breast.

Sparrows, snowfinches and accentors

The commonest sparrow in China is the tree sparrow (*Passer montanus*), which is found throughout the country, including in urban areas. Also quite common in central and southern regions is the russet sparrow (*P. rutilans*), which has brighter plumage. Snowfinches (*Montifringilla* and *Pyrgilauda*) are sparrow-like birds of the high mountains and plateaux. They have obvious white patches and white outer tail feathers, and can be quite tame and approachable. Accentors are also rather sparrow-like, though not closely related. The alpine accentor (*Prunella collaris*) inhabits alpine meadows and scrub in north and west China.

Like most seedeaters, crossbills drink frequently. (DMc)

Finches and buntings

The finches and buntings are a large family with about 80 species in China, including several species of rosefinch, for which China is the global centre of distribution. Here we can only mention a few members. The grey-capped greenfinch (*Carduelis sinica*) is common over the eastern half of the country in varied habitats, including parks and gardens. Pink-winged and sandy coloured, the desert finch (*Rhodospiza obsoleta*) is a bird of the deserts of the north and northwest, while the common crossbill (*Loxia curvirostra*) breeds in the pine forests of the northeast. The rosefinches (*Carpodacus*) are rather confusing; they have streaked plumage, suffused with pink in the male, while the females of most are a drab grey-brown. The common rosefinch (*C. erythrinus*) is a widespread species of subalpine forests. The pale rosefinch (*C. synoicus*) is a pretty species of the arid mountains of the northwest. Sandy-coloured and unstreaked, the male has a rose-pink breast. Centred on the Tibetan Plateau, three further species are quite common. The beautiful rosefinch (*C. pulcherrimus*) is mainly brown with a pinkish breast (male); the slightly larger white-browed rosefinch (*C. thura*) is pinker below and with a white spot near the back of its head; larger still is the red-fronted rosefinch (*C. puniceus*) with (male) robin-like red breast and a pink rump. All are high-altitude birds, and the latter even breeds at above 5,500m.

The grey-headed bullfinch (*Pyrrhula erythaca*), with grey head and back and orange breast and belly in the male, is found in subalpine forests of central China, while the all grey and black brown bullfinch (*P. nipalensis*) tends to replace it in the south. The yellow-billed grosbeak (*Eophona migratoria*) is a large woodland finch of central and northeast regions. It has a large bill, yellow with a black tip. Two further grosbeaks, white-winged (*Mycerobas carnipes*) and collared (*M. affinis*), live in mountain forests of central and western China. Both are mainly black and yellow, the latter mainly yellow, with a black (male) or grey (female) head.

One of the commoner small buntings is the black-faced bunting (*Emberiza spodocephala*), found in scrub and woods in central and northeast China. The somewhat larger chestnut-eared bunting (*E. fucata*) has a grey crown and chestnut ear coverts. The yellow-breasted bunting (*E. aureola*) is common in reeds, crops and damp scrub in the northeast. The male is quite striking: yellow below, with a black face and chestnut nape. Godlewski's bunting (*E. godlewskii*) is a large bunting with grey, brown-striped head, and is found typically on rocky hills and scrubland; it has a scattered distribution from the Tian Shan foothills, south to northern Yunnan. Locally common in the bushy steppes of the far northwest is the red-headed bunting (*E. bruniceps*); it is yellow, with green back and red head and neck. Lastly, mention should be made of the charming endemic Tibetan bunting (*E. koslowi*). The male is grey, with chestnut back, black and white face and a pure white bib.

REPTILES,
AMPHIBIANS AND FISH

The venomous long-nosed pit viper has a horn on the tip of its snout.

O f the approximately 7,780 known reptile species, China boasts about 400, and the country's many waterways mean that it also has an impressive diversity of amphibians and freshwater fish. Observing these animals may not always be straightforward but it is immensely rewarding.

REPTILES

Reptiles are distinguished from amphibians by their dry skin covered in scales. China's 400 species comprise some 350 lizards and snakes, nearly 40 turtles and tortoises, and a single crocodilian – the Chinese alligator.

SNAKES

While the majority of China's roughly 200 snake species are harmless, a handful are dangerously venomous.

Venomous snakes

These include Ursini's viper (*Vipera ursinii*) from Xinjiang and common adder (*V. berus*) from northeast China, as well as pit vipers and cobras in the south. The

Top Monocled cobra showing monocle pattern behind the head.
Above The king cobra has a neurotoxin venom.

monocled cobra (*Naja kaouthia*) and king cobra (*Ophiophagus hannah*) can still be found in the tropical south, but both have declined through hunting. The king cobra is the world's largest venomous snake, growing to an impressive 6m, and feeds almost entirely on other snakes. It can also be aggressive, especially when guarding its eggs. Other venomous snakes are the banded kraits (*Bungarus fasciatus* and *B. multicinctus*), Jerdon's pit viper (*Trimeresurus jerdonii*) and the green tree viper (*T. stejnegeri*). The kraits are among the most dangerous snakes because they are fairly widespread, especially in southwest China, and may occur near rice paddies. Their bites can be fatal. The green tree viper is a common snake in southern China. Bright green, it is well disguised in woodland or bamboo and is often found along streams and also near villages. The sunbeam snake (*Xenopeltis unicolor*) has scales so smooth that they produce shimmering colours as they reflect the sunlight. It is a shy species of tropical regions.

Constrictors

China's largest snake is the Burmese python (*Python molurus*), a constricting snake that can grow to a length of 7m. This impressive reptile inhabits the tropical south, notably Yunnan, and is at home both in the trees and in water, feeding mainly on mammals, birds and their eggs. It has sadly suffered persecution for its skin, and is now much rarer than it used to be.

Rat snakes and others

The rat snakes (mainly the genus *Elaphe*) are widespread non-venomous snakes. China has several species. The mandarin rat snake (*E. mandarina*) grows to about 1m and is boldly marked with black and yellow diamond-shaped patches. It is often found near houses and feeds largely on rodents and lizards. The similar-sized black-banded trinket snake (*E. porphyracea*) is also quite abundant. It is brownish with widely spaced dark bands. The Chinese rat snake (*Zaocys dhumnades*) is widespread in plains, hills and low mountains, and often searches for rodents or frogs in rice paddies. Rather drab brown, it grows to 2.5m. This relatively common species is widely used in traditional medicine. It is also caught to be eaten, snake meat being regarded locally as a delicacy.

The beauty snake (*E. taeniura*) grows to 2m and, although non-venomous, can be aggressive. It is often found near villages and in cultivated fields. More dangerous is the red-necked keelback (*Rhabdophis subminiatus*), which is often found in rice fields and around streams and ponds. It is mildly venomous and feeds mainly on frogs, toads and other small vertebrates. It is uniformly grey-green except for the neck and front of the body, which are red. The big-eyed bamboo snake (*Pseudoxenodon macrops*) is an unusual species. It is dark above and pale yellow beneath. Although non-venomous, it has an alarming threat display, which mimics that of a cobra, as it raises the front of its body and flattens its neck.

The Asian green vinesnake (*Ahaetulla prasina*) deserves a mention. This is a remarkable species from the tropical forests of southern and western Yunnan. It is bright green, with a pencil-thin body up to 2m long, a long head and a pointed snout. Beautifully camouflaged, and venomous though not deadly, it lurks hidden amongst the foliage then strikes rapidly to catch small lizards, frogs or birds.

Top The Chinese green tree viper is primarily arboreal.
Above The red-necked keelback is common in Beijing.

LIZARDS

China's lizards include lacertids (familiar in Europe and Africa), as well as geckos, skinks, and the rather less familiar agamids, and the largest of all, the powerful monitor lizards (*Varanus*).

Lacertid lizards

The lacertids are represented by, for example, the grass lizards (*Takydromus*). These are rather small lizards, some of which are found even in the north, where they hibernate to avoid the cold winters.

Agamid lizards

Agamids are large-headed lizards and include the imaginatively named bloodsuckers, dragons, mountain lizards and flying dragons. The common bloodsucker (*Calotes versicolor*) is abundant in scrub, woods and grassland in the south. Its body is about 10cm long, with a tail almost three times as long. Usually brown-grey, the male develops a bright red head and neck in the breeding season, which explains the common name. The deserts of northern China are home to toad-headed lizards (*Phrynocephalus*) of which there are about 18 species. Long-tailed and large-headed, these cryptically patterned lizards scurry about amongst the sand and rocks. The Yunnan mountain lizard (*Japalura yunnanensis*) is endemic to the highlands of western Yunnan, between about 1800 and 2000m. It is grey-brown and has a low crest running along its back. The most unusual of China's agamid lizards are the flying dragons (*Draco*). The spotted flying dragon (*D. maculatus*) is about 20cm long including the tail and inhabits the forests of south west Yunnan. The first five ribs of flying dragons are long and moveable, and connected by a thin flap of skin forming a wing-like structure enabling the lizard to glide as it leaps. The Chinese water dragon (*Physignathus cocincinus*) is one of the largest of the agamids, growing to 90cm, of which about two thirds is tail. It is usually greenish-grey, but can change shade in the manner of a chameleon. Found in the tropical south, it is semi-aquatic and feeds mainly on insects and also small fish. It is also an agile climber and spends much of its time in the branches of trees.

Geckos and skinks

Geckos are fairly common in the warmer regions, and some may be seen running up the walls of houses, especially close to lights, which attract moths and other insects. The largest, at about 30cm, is the Tokay gecko (*Gekko gecko*) which uses its Velcro-like flat footpads to adhere to even the smoothest surfaces. It is found mainly in the south, from Yunnan east to Fujian.

Other southern geckos include the stump-toed gecko (*Gehydra mutilata*) and the small tree gecko (*Hemiphyllodactylus typus*), both small species that have sharp claws rather than footpads to cling to rocks, bark and walls. Skinks are small lizards with smooth scales and usually flat heads and short limbs. The writhing skink (*Lygosoma indicum*) is a southern species, common in grassy areas, even in parks, while the mountain ground skink (*Scincella monticola*) lives in high-altitude grassland.

The Chinese water dragon is a good swimmer.

The Asiatic monitor is at home on land and in the water.

Monitor lizards

The monitors are the largest of all lizards. They are active by day and find their prey by tasting the scent in the air using their long, sensitive tongues. They feed on a wide range of prey – including rodents, birds, other reptiles, fish, amphibians and invertebrates. The Asiatic monitor (*Varanus salvator*) can reach over 2m. Along with the Chinese alligator this reptile may be responsible for inspiring stories of the legendary Chinese dragon. Equally at home on land, in the trees or in water, this splendid lizard is found mainly in the southern provinces of Yunnan, Guangxi, Guangdong and Hainan. Its tail is laterally compressed to aid swimming, it even sometimes swims out to sea. Monitor lizards can run well and if necessary they will flail their long, muscular tails in defence.

TURTLES AND TORTOISES (CHELONIANS)

About 40 species of chelonian are found in China, out of a global total of about 300. The majority of China's turtles and tortoises are found in the southern regions, with the freshwater turtles the most diverse.

Soft-shelled turtles

Several species of soft-shelled turtle are found in China, inhabiting rivers, lakes and ponds. These species feed mainly on fish and aquatic invertebrates such as shrimps and crabs. The Asian giant soft-shelled turtle (*Pelochelys bibroni*) is a magnificent reptile reaching 80cm long and 65cm across, with fully grown individuals tipping the scales at 70kg. Endangered, mainly through over-hunting, it lives in rivers and lakes, mainly in central and southern Yunnan. The smaller Chinese soft-shelled turtle (*Pelodiscus sinensis*) is much commoner, ranging over most of China, with the exception of Tibet and the far northwest. It has a long tube-like snout and extensible neck. This is the species most likely to be seen, but dishearteningly your first sight of it may well be in a tank at the entrance to a restaurant or food store, as the Chinese consider soft-shelled turtles a special delicacy!

Chinese soft-shelled turtles feed on freshwater life.

Turtles and tortoises have long been regarded as important in Chinese culture, partly as symbols of strength and longevity, but also as food and medicine. This has led to massive over-exploitation of wild populations and even large-scale importing from neighbouring countries of southeast Asia. Historically, turtles were also caught and exported for the pet market, posing yet another threat to the wild populations.

The elongate tortoise has an unusually long, narrow shell.

The Chinese soft-shelled turtle is now also farmed extensively to supply the domestic trade but wild turtles are still under pressure and many are threatened.

The albino form of the Chinese soft-shelled turtle is a popular pet.

Other freshwater turtles

There are also small turtles whose bodies approach those of tortoises in shape, and these live partly in streams, mainly in mountain regions. Examples are the Asian leaf turtle and Mouhot's leaf turtle (*Cyclemys dentata* and *C. mouhotii*) and the related black-breasted leaf turtle (*Geoemyda spengleri*). The latter two species are semi-aquatic, and their feet are only weakly webbed. The shell of the black-breasted leaf turtle has three obvious ridges and is sharply serrated at the back. The southeast Asian box turtle (*Cuora amboinensis*) has a high-domed smooth shell. It lives mainly in ponds and rivers, but is also found in swamps and rice paddies.

Perhaps the strangest of all China's turtles is the big-headed turtle (*Platysternon megacephalum*), classed in a family all of its own. Well-named, its head is very large and equipped with a fearsome-looking hooked beak, like a bird of prey. It also has a long, muscular tail; neither head nor tail can be pulled into the shell. Its behaviour is odd too; it lives in or near mountain streams and is quite capable of clambering into the branches.

Asian box turtles are also well-known in the pet trade.

A green turtle underwater, showing its distinctive shell pattern. (AN)

Adult green turtles feed on marine grasses and algae. (JC)

Marine turtles

Marine turtles still breed at a handful of beaches, but these are mainly in the clusters of islands in the South China Sea. One mainland site, Huidong on the Guangdong coast, has a special reserve for marine turtles where thousands of green seaturtles (*Chelonia mydas*) come ashore to lay their eggs.

Tortoises

Terrestrial tortoises include the elongate tortoise (*Indotestudo elongata*), a herbivore found in tropical and subtropical regions, and the larger brown tortoise (*Manouria impressa*), which reaches a length of about 30cm and almost the same width. The elongate tortoise has a pale yellow head and a grey-green shell and is found mainly in hilly country of the south. The shell of the brown tortoise has serrated edges to the front of its brown shell. The central Asian tortoise (*Testudo horsfieldii*) is a rare species occuring only in the northwest, where it finds protection in a special reserve in Xinjiang. It escapes the summer heat by retiring to its burrow, and hibernates during the harsh winters.

CROCODILIANS

Crocodilians are the largest living reptiles. The 23 species of crocodile, alligator and their relatives are mostly confined to the tropics and subtropics. Powerful, with streamlined bodies and thick, scaly skin, these fierce predators have strong jaws lined with sharp teeth.

Chinese alligator (*Alligator sinensis*)

This relatively small, endemic alligator is now very rare. Once widely distributed throughout the eastern Yangtze River system in China, it is today mostly restricted to a 433km² reserve in Anhui Province. Any wild populations that remain are severely fragmented and almost none exist in their natural habitat. However, the Chinese government has recently allocated funds to create new habitats with a view to introducing captive-bred alligators into the wild in three other provinces.

The Chinese alligator has played a major role in the folklore and culture of China – not least because it almost certainly gave rise to the myth of the dragon – a fierce-looking mysterious reptilian predator capable of moving rapidly from land to water and associated with wetlands and hence with rainstorms. Yet persecution and habitat destruction have combined to bring this charismatic reptile to the very brink of total extinction. Its loss would be not only an international scandal, it would also be a tremendous blow to the Chinese character – China without its dragon is unthinkable!

ALLIGATOR CONSERVATION

The Chinese alligator was once quite common through many of China's river systems, but drainage, hunting and poisoning (mainly via poisoned rats that the alligators then eat) over many years have taken their toll, with the result that this charismatic species now stands at the brink of extinction in the wild. Classed as critically endangered, it is the world's rarest species of crocodilian. Today there are probably only about 150 wild alligators left, in pools and tributaries in the lower Yangtze valley.

The good news is that they are fairly easy to breed in captivity and many thousands have been bred in zoos, especially at the Special Alligator Research Centre in Anhui. Conservation efforts began in earnest in 1979, and the numbers in captivity now stand at more than 10,000. Trials of releasing alligators into suitable habitats have been undertaken, and the results are gratifyingly encouraging. The captive-bred animals seem to adapt very quickly to their natural habitats and to thrive there in their new-found freedom. The plan is to release 1,000 alligators into existing or restored wetlands over the next few years. At the same time, the habitats of the existing small wild populations will be improved, and new wetlands created.

Very few Chinese alligators are now left in the wild.

Four sites within the National Chinese Alligator Reserve have been earmarked as offering the best potential for establishing small breeding groups of alligators: Hongxin and Zhaungtou (Xuancheng County), and Zhongqiao and Shaungken (Jinxiang County). Some of the surrounding rice paddies will be converted into more natural wetlands, with guaranteed minimum water levels all year round. This work will require parallel efforts to educate local people about the importance of the alligators, and may perhaps involve allowing the collection of a certain percentage of juvenile alligators for sale to breeding centres or to other communities that want to establish alligators in their own ponds.

Chinese fire-bellied newts sport a vibrant orange and brown belly.

AMPHIBIANS

Of the global total of more than 5,500 species of amphibian, China has about 300. Frogs and toads constitute the majority of amphibians (China has about 200 from a global total of about 4,750, the majority tropical or subtropical), but the group also contains newts, salamanders and the strange, worm-like caecilians. Although few amphibians are fully aquatic as adults, most live in or close to water for much of their lives, and most have aquatic larvae. Caecilians, of which China has but one species, have cylindrical, limbless bodies and reduced eyes, and spend most of their lives burrowing below ground. Many of the frogs live in trees. Most amphibians are dormant during climatically stressful periods – hibernating during cold winter weather, or aestivating during hot dry periods in warmer regions. As for so many other groups, Yunnan is the richest province for amphibians, boasting about 112 species, 30 of which are endemic.

CAECILIANS AND SALAMANDERS

These amphibians lack the leaping powers of the frogs and toads and so are more closely tied to water or (in the case of caecilians) the soil. They make up just a small proportion of China's amphibian fauna.

Banna caecilian (*Ichthyophis bannanicus*)

The Banna caecilian is China's only representative of this unusual group. It lives close to small streams in the tropical region of Xishuangbanna in southern Yunnan, and in southern Guangxi and Guangdong. It grows to about 40cm and its tiny eyes are buried below the skin. The larvae are aquatic, but the adults live in moist soil and feed on insect larvae and worms.

Newts and salamanders

Many of China's 36 species of newt and salamander are endemic. Crocodile newts (*Tylototriton*) live in mountain streams and ponds, or underneath leaves or logs. They take their name from the crocodile-like rows of warts and ridges along their back. Some are brightly coloured: the Shanjing crocodile newt (*T. shanjing*), from west Yunnan, is bright orange, while the Kweichow crocodile newt (*T. kweichowensis*), from Guizhou and Yunnan, has a black head and orange and black longitudinal stripes along its body. The Chinese firebellied newt (*Cynops orientalis*) is found mainly in the eastern lowlands, where it is sometimes seen in rice paddies. Dark brown above, it has bright red irregular spots on the underside.

The Chinese giant salamander (*Andrias davidianus*) is one of China's most extraordinary animals. It is the world's largest amphibian, growing to more than a metre, sometimes even to 1.7m, and weighing more than 60kg. It has a large, flat head and its rather rubbery body is patterned black and orange. Giant salamanders live in clear mountain streams, mainly between about 300 and 800m. They rest in holes in the bank or in rock crevices, and are entirely aquatic. They make a noise rather like a baby's cry, giving them the local name 'baby fish', and they can live for at least 50 years. Like so many of China's wild animals, giant salamanders are threatened by collection, mainly for food, and are said to taste delicious!

The Chinese giant salamander is a prehistoric-looking beast with a huge head.

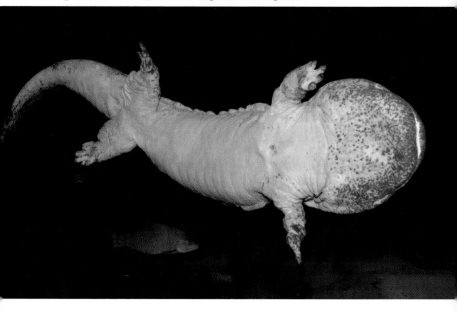

FROGS

China has a large and diverse frog fauna, with several distinct groups represented and a number of endemic species.

True frogs

One of the commonest of the Ranidae or true frogs is the rice frog (*Rana limnocharis*), which is often abundant in rice paddies and in other wetlands. It is grey-brown and has a clear yellow-green stripe running down the centre of its back. Another common frog of central and southern China is Günther's frog (*R. guentheri*). It is found in a range of wetland habitats, from pools and paddy fields to ditches and slow streams, and is often collected for food. Günther's frog has a greenish-yellow back and a dark band along its sides. The black-spotted pond frog (*R. nigromaculata*) is common in ponds and ditches, mainly in northern China. This noisy frog has black spots and a green stripe down the centre of its back.

Günther's frog in Diaoluoshan NP on Hainan Island.

The spiny frog (*Paa spinosa*) is a large frog found across central and southern China, including Hong Kong. It lives mainly in rocky streams in evergreen forest, and like so many others has suffered from over-collection for food. The wrinkled frog or Chinese bullfrog (*R. rugulosa*) is large and found in southern China, in ponds and also in rice paddies. It has a yellow stripe down its back and pale green wrinkled skin with dark green blotches. Anderson's frog and Graham's frog (*R. andersoni* and *R. grahami*) are similar species that live around mountain streams in the southwest. These two frogs are both bright green, with yellow sides and legs, and both have declined through over-collection.

One of the prettiest of tropical frogs is the green cascade frog (*R. livida*), found in the south, including southern Yunnan and Hong Kong. It has a broad emerald green stripe along its back and lives in and around well-vegetated streams. The sucker frog (*Amolops viridimaculatus*) is a rare species found only in the Gaoligongshan, Ailao Shan and Wuliang Shan of Yunnan. It too is a pretty frog, patterned with pale green spots on a brown background. The pads on its feet help it get a secure grip on rocks and pebbles in mountain streams. Much commoner is the closely related *A. wuyiensis*, from Fujian, Anhui and Zhejiang.

Another interesting tropical group are the floating frogs (*Occidozyga*). The pointed-tongued floating frog (*O. lima*) and Marten's frog (*O. martensii*) are found in tropical China in small ponds, slow streams and paddies. Greenish-brown, plump and buoyant, they habitually float on the water's surface, then dive down quickly when disturbed.

Narrow-mouthed frogs

The mainly tropical Microhylidae or narrow-mouthed frogs are mostly very small, and many are really tiny. They are found in grass near ditches and ponds and also in rice paddies, in southern China. Butler's frog (*Microhyla butleri*), a common species of forest edges and cultivated fields, measures less than 3cm, and is brown with a white belly. The ornate rice frog (*M. ornata*) and the Guangdong rice frog (*M. pulchra*) are both about 3cm long and also quite widespread in the south. They are grey-brown with quite intricate darker bands. These bands form a distinctive V-shape on the back of the Guangdong rice frog. They feed mainly on small insects, including small butterflies and moths. Even more prettily marked is the slightly larger and mainly terrestrial Sumatra grainy frog (*Kalophrynus pleurostigma*). It is pinkish-grey with darker parallel V-markings on its back.

Tree frogs

The tree frogs (Hylidae) are slender with long limbs and often green, yellow or brown. They have adhesive discs on their toes to help them climb on smooth leaves. Chinese tree frog (*Hyla chinensis*) is a common species of central and eastern China in vegetation around pools, while *H. annectans* is the common tree frog of the southwest, where it is found in grassland, pools and paddies.

Afro-Asian tree frogs

Frogs of the family Rhacophoridae, known as whipping frogs, are graceful, long-legged, slim frogs that spend much of their time in trees and waterside vegetation. The brown tree frog (*Polypedates megacephalus*) is widespread in central, southern and southwest China, including Hainan and Hong Kong. The related Burmese whipping frog (*P. mutus*), which is a lighter shade of brown, is found mainly in southern and western Yunnan, Guizhou and Guangxi.

This family also contains the amazing 'flying' frogs. Evolution has adapted their webbed feet into mini-parachutes, enabling them to extend their leaps by gliding through the air. The Yunnan flying frog (*Rhacophorus rhodopus*) is very small, only about 4cm long, and grey-brown, while the Gongshan flying frog (*R. gongshanensis*), restricted to the Gaoligong range in western Yunnan, is about twice the size and

The brown tree frog is an agile climber.

bright green with yellow spots. Larger still, at about 10cm, is Reinwardt's flying frog (*R. reinwardtii*). It is green above and yellow below, with purple-black webbing 'parachutes' on each foot. Flying frogs lay their eggs inside nests of bubbly foam on the leaves of waterside plants. When the tadpoles hatch they drop into the water below. The tiny bubble-nest frog (*Philautus cavirostris*) also occurs in southern Yunnan. Only about 4cm long, it has serrated folds of skin on its forearms and feet, and it produces a ringing call.

Reinwardt's flying frog glides by spreading its webbed toes.

TOADS

This is another large and well-represented group of amphibians, although from a taxonomic point of view they are not distinct from frogs – both frogs and toads belong to the Anura order.

True toads

The Bufonidae or true toads are also well-represented in China. They have very warty skin and short limbs. Andrew's toad (*Bufo andrewsi*) is found in western China, and is common in rice fields and ponds, especially in the southwest. The black-spined (black-spectacled) toad (*B. melanostictus*) is a common toad of the south. It is quite large, growing to about 20cm, its warts have black spines, and it also has black ridges around its eyes and along its nose. The Mongolian toad (*B. raddei*) is a small species found mainly in the north, in a wide range of habitats, from forest to steppe. It is olive green, with darker spots. The Tibetan toad (*B. tibetanus*) is very decorative, patterned in orange, black and white with a grey stripe down its back. It lives near streams and under rocks and in alpine grassland in the highlands of Tibet, Qinghai, Sichuan and Yunnan, between about 2,000 and 4,300m, where it is quite common.

The Oriental fire-bellied toad has dramatic warning colours on its belly.

Firebellied and bell toads

Toads of this genus (*Bombina*) are found in many areas. The Oriental firebellied toad (*B. orientalis*) is mainly found in the northeast, while the related large-webbed bell toad (*B. maxima*) is from southwest China, found in Sichuan, Yunnan and Guizhou between 2,000 and 3,600m. In both of these species the very warty skin is green and brown on the back with patches of bright orange-red on the underside.

Asian toadfrogs

The Megophryidae is an unusual family, a group that blurs the arbitrary distinction between frogs and toads. The Asian horned toadfrog (*Megophrys lateralis*), which is found in upland streams, has large eyes with horn-like projections above them, and a white band along the jaw. The most bizarre of China's amphibians also belongs to this family – the spiny or moustached toad (*Vibrissaphora ailaonica*). This toad has complex ridges on its body and the upper jaw of the male is armed with a row of sharp hard spines. The large eyes are divided horizontally and are black in the lower half, bright green above. This rare amphibian is found in the Ailao Shan and Wuliang Shan ranges in Yunnan, between about 2,000 and 2,500m.

The Asian horned toadfrog has a pointed 'horn' above each eye, which serves to enhance its camouflage on the forest floor.

FISH

In a country blessed with so many lakes and rivers, China's fish fauna is understandably diverse. We can therefore only mention here a small selection of the more interesting or unusual species.

WILD FISH

Many of China's wetlands suffer from pollution, especially the lower reaches of the main rivers and their nearby tributaries and lakes, and fish, being sensitive indicators of water quality, are often badly affected.

Some common lake and river fish

The grass carp (*Ctenopharyngodon idella*) is a herbivorous fish, native to northern China. It is widely reared for food and is well known around the world as it has been introduced to a number of other countries to control aquatic weeds. Chinese snakehead (*Channa asiatica*) is a large predatory fish from southern China, growing to more than 1m and inhabiting sluggish waters. It can also move overland for short distances. The Wuchang bream (*Megalobrama amblycephala*) is another freshwater fish, from the middle reaches of the Yangtze River and nearby lakes. Like several other fish, it is widely farmed, often kept within submerged bamboo-framed polythene cages.

Grass carp feed on aquatic plants.

The Chinese sturgeon's mouth barbels enable it to feel its way along the bottom.

Localised and scarce fish

The Mekong giant catfish (*Pangasianodon gigas*) is southeast Asia's biggest and rarest fish, growing to 3m and nearly 300kg, making it one of the world's largest freshwater fish. These giant herbivores browse plants and algae and are occasionally seen in the Lancang (Mekong) River, though numbers have dwindled. Another giant is the Chinese paddlefish (*Psephurus gladius*), once found in the middle Yangtze River area, but now seen so infrequently that it may already be extinct. This sturgeon relative has a long snout and can grow to 2m or more.

The Chinese sturgeon (*Acipenser sinensis*) is an endemic species confined to the Yangtze River and perhaps also once in the Pearl River and Yellow River. It is a large fish that spawns upstream in the autumn. It has proved popular both for its flesh and also its roe (caviar). The spawning sites are often sections of the river with steep cliffs on both banks, rock-choked riverbeds with deep pools, and turbulent currents and open gravel beaches below them. The fertilised eggs sink and stick to the gravel

The Chinese sucker has outsized lips.

before hatching. The young fry then descend the river to the sea where they feed mainly at the sea-floor. The species has become threatened, especially during the last two decades, mainly after the Gezhouba Reservoir dammed the Yangtze River and blocked the channel for the fish to swim back from the sea. Artificial breeding and release programmes have been successful, and a large spawning site has been set up in the Dujiang section of the river below the dam, so the future for this splendid fish is now looking brighter.

The Chinese sucker is found mainly in the Yangtze River.

Chinese sucker (*Myxocyprinus asiaticus*) is adapted to live in fast currents and has a compressed body and sucker-like mouth. It is found only in the Jinsha and Yangtze River systems. Bronze gudgeon (*Coreius guichenoti*) is another fish of fast rivers, mainly in the Jinsha Jiang. A large fish, growing to 4kg, it uses its sensitive barbels to help locate its food from the riverbed.

The spiny barbel (*Spinibarbus yunannensis*) is a fish from Fuxian Lake, now endangered by over-fishing, with just a small population remaining.

Blind cave fish in Yunnan's Jiuxiang Cave.

Cave fish

China also has several species of cave fish, adapted to live in the dark waters of the many underground caves and caverns, notably in the karst regions of the south. The Gejiu blind loach (*Tryplophysa gejiuensis*) is one such. It inhabits underground rivers in Gejiu, Yunnan. Colourless, and lacking scales, it is totally blind, tracking its prey by detecting

123

vibrations. Another group of cave fish, also endemic to China, are the golden-line fish (*Sinocyclocheilus*), found in certain caves in Yunnan. They are almost or totally blind and have a domed head, some with a projection, that is thought to contain a non-visual sensory organ. Their diet includes bat droppings!

FISH FARMED OR COLLECTED FOR FOOD

The Chinese eat a wide range of wild fish, and in some cases, notably among local endemic species, this has created severe conservation problems. Partly to meet demand, but also in an effort to protect wild stocks, the emphasis is now more and more on fish-farming, either in ponds created for that purpose, or in cages lowered into rivers and lakes.

Golden-line barbel (*Anabarilius grahami*)

The endemic golden-line barbel is found only in Fuxian Lake in Yunnan. Small and silvery, it feeds on planktonic invertebrates in the clear waters of this lake, which reaches a depth of 155m. These fish have been harvested as food by locals, who exploit the fact that they are attracted to turbulent water. Currents are created, and bell-shaped bamboo baskets positioned such that the schooling fish are trapped and then easily harvested.

Snow-trout

Lugu Lake, another deep natural lake, set in a landscape of pine-covered highlands at about 2,400m in northern Yunnan, supports three endemic species of fish in the genus *Schizothorax*, including the thick lip (*S. labrosus*). These fish, often known as snow-trout, are trout-like in shape and are characterised by their minute scales. Other snow-trout species are found in the Jinsha Jiang and its tributaries.

The bizarre-looking Chinese snakehead is an aggressive carnivore.

INVERTEBRATES

The monarch butterfly has a toxic
body derived from its larval diet.

A round 97% of all known animals are invertebrates, the most diverse group of which is the insects, with more than a million species known to science. For the visiting naturalist it is in the warmer southern regions that insects and other invertebrates are most often encountered: the province of Yunnan alone has around 100,000 species of insect. In this book we can do no more than scratch the surface of this vast array, but I have mentioned here some of the better-known groups and examples.

BUTTERFLIES AND MOTHS

With a global total of around 200,000 species, the butterflies and moths (order Lepidoptera) are such a large group that we can only mention a representative selection of China's diversity. The southern provinces have the most species, many of which are large and colourful. Yunnan Province alone for example has about 600, an impressive total indeed when compared with Britain's 60 species!

Swallowtails

One important and prominent group of tropical butterflies are the Papilionidae or swallowtails. The common swallowtail (*Papilio machaon*), familiar from Europe, is quite common in northern China. Southern China, however, has several even larger members of this family. These large, showy insects, often with 'tail streamers' on their hind wings, can be seen gliding bird-like over forest clearings or at streamsides, often alighting to drink and take in minerals from wet sand or animal droppings.

The furry-bodied apollo butterfly is a mountain species. (FT)

One of the most beautiful is the Paris peacock (*Achillides paris*), whose larvae feed on citrus. This splendid insect has an impressive 13cm wingspan and displays bright iridescent spots on the hind wings. The forewings are gracefully curved and dark, speckled green. Look for it in the forests of southern Yunnan, though it is quite widespread in other parts of central and southern China.

Also from southern China is the Krishna peacock (*Papilio krishna*) and the very similar blue peacock (*P. arcturus*). These are large, dark swallowtails with broad, spoon-shaped tails. Their wings are mainly black, but have a powdering of green scales and an area of blue and purple spots on the hindwings. Another southern species is the common mormon (*P. polytes*), which is black with white marginal spots. The great mormon (*P. memnon*) is one of the largest of China's swallowtails, with a span of 15cm. It is mainly grey and white, with red patches at the base of the forewings. The larvae of this fine swallowtail feed on citrus bushes. Another distinctive swallowtail is the glassy bluebottle (*Graphium cloanthus*), which is about

Top Paris peacock in Yunnan.
Above Common rose feeding on *Lantana*.

10cm across and has black-edged greenish-blue wings, with sharply pointed tails. Both wings have pale green, translucent spots and patches.

The Asian (Chinese yellow) swallowtail (*P. xuthus*) is also found further north, and is on the wing from May through August. It is mainly black, with yellow stripes and spots and a single tail to each hindwing. The common rose (*Pachliopta aristolochiae*) is found in eastern China. It is mainly black, with red and white spots and a tail on each hindwing. The Gifu butterfly (*Luehdorfia chinensis*) is bright yellow with tiger-like black stripes and short tails. It lives mainly in the lower Yangtze region, and the larvae feed on *Asarum*.

The great nawab (*Polyura eudamippus*) is another swallowtail, this time from eastern China. Its wings are creamy white with black margins. Golden Kaiser (*Teinopalpus aureus*) is a splendid endemic swallowtail with a scalloped hindwing. It is brown and green with large golden patches on the hindwings of the male, and found locally in the southern provinces, notably at Wuyishan on the Jiangxi/Fujian border. The Apollo or parnassid butterflies also belong to this family. These hardy

The boldly marked common tiger butterfly adds colour to the forest.

butterflies are typical of upland and mountain regions and there are about 30 species in China, including the Apollo (*Parnassius apollo*), which is restricted to Xinjiang. The small Apollo (*P. phoebus*) is more widespread, mainly in the north, flying from June to September. It has white, partly transparent wings with black and red spots. One of the most remarkable of the parnassids is the three-tailed Bhutan glory (*Butanitis [Sinonitis] thaidina*). It has a wingspan of 10cm and is black with thin cream stripes, but its most impressive feature are the triple tails on each hindwing, giving it the look of a swallowtail. It lives above about 2,000m, in Yunnan, Sichuan, Tibet and Shanxi. The larval host is *Aristolochia*.

One group of tropical papilionids is known as the birdwings, because of their large size and long forewings. The golden birdwing (*Troides aeacus*) is the most northerly of this group and is found in the tropical south. A magnificent insect, its wingspan reaches 17cm and the black forewings contrast boldly with its golden yellow hindwings as it swoops and glides in forest clearings. Like many brightly coloured insects, it is distasteful to predators, and its yellow and black colours warn birds not to attack.

Brush-footed butterflies

The family Nymphalidae is also known as the brush-footed butterflies, as their first pair of legs are tiny, hairy stumps held against the body. This large family has many members in China. Japanese emperor (*Sasakia charonda*) is a large nymphalid, resembling the purple emperor of Europe, but, at 12cm wingspan, rather larger. Even more closely related to the latter is *Apatura schrenkii* from north China.

The red lacewing (*Cethosia biblis*) is a common butterfly of southern woodlands. The underwing is prettily patterned with black, yellow, white and red bands.

The related *C. cyane* is similarly patterned, but is mainly black and white and is one of the commoner butterflies of the subtropical and tropical lowlands. Its larvae feed on passionflowers.

Some Chinese butterflies are good leaf mimics, particularly when resting with their wings closed. One such is the orange oakleaf (*Kallima inachis*), which is widespread in central and southern China. The inner surfaces of its wings are brown and orange, with a purplish-blue sheen, but the outer surfaces resemble a dead leaf and even have markings mimicking central and lateral

The orange oakleaf butterfly blends into the forest floor.

leaf veins. Another nymphalid butterfly with a cryptically patterned underside is the jungle queen (*Stichophthalma louisa*). It often gathers in swarms in bamboo forests, or to lick up minerals from the ground near tropical streams. The larvae feed on bamboo and can sometimes reach plague numbers, causing considerable damage to the bamboo plants.

The common map (*Cyrestis thyodamas*) is another butterfly from central and southern regions. Its wings are pale white and partly translucent, giving it a strange, ghostly appearance. It is well camouflaged when alighted on limestone rocks. Its range is from Tibet east to Zhejiang and south to Hainan. The common tiger or milkweed (*Salatura genutia*) is quite a widespread medium-sized species, especially in lowland sites. It has bold orange and black markings and bright white spots, and these advertise the fact that its body contains poisons. The chestnut tiger (*Parantica sita*) has long, rather narrow wings, spread horizontally, to about 12cm across. The forewings are blue and black, and the hindwings a bright chestnut red.

The grey baron (*Euthalia anosia*) is fairly widespread in the south, but is somewhat local; the larvae feed on mangos. Its upperside is brown with white spots and the underside grey, giving good camouflage against bark and rocks. The fritillaries belong to this family and some familiar species from Europe also occur in northern China, such as the splendid silver-washed fritillary (*Argynnis paphia*) with its silvery hindwing.

Blues, metalmarks, hairstreaks and skippers

Many of the smaller butterflies of the region belong to the families Lycaenidae (blues and their allies) and Hesperiidae (skippers), but a specialist guide would be required for accurate identification of these. One of the prettiest of the skippers is *Choaspes benjaminii*, which has brown and metallic blue forewings with a light green base, and bright orange tips to the hindwings. This is a species of mountain forests in south and southwest China. The hairstreak *Heliophorus saphir* is another pretty butterfly. The male has shiny blue wings, tipped in black, and the hindwings have

A black-veined white butterfly feeds on an alpine flower.

bright orange along the trailing edge. The long-banded silverline (*Spindasis lohita*) is metallic blue above and yellow with red stripes below. The hindwings have curled tails and a red patch, creating a false head. When the insect is at rest it twitches the tails, thus diverting the attantion of any potential predator away from the vulnerable parts of its body.

Whites and relatives

Butterflies of the family Pieridae are often referred to as 'whites', although not all species are white. They are also well represented in China, and include the large white (*Pieris brassicae*), one of the most familiar of all butterflies. The genus *Delias* is represented by several large southern species. They are almost completely black, with scattered pale spots and yellow patches on the hindwings. Another white is *Aporia hippia*, a pretty species of mountain sites in the south, with dark-veined creamy white wings. Its larvae feed on barberry (*Berberis*). *Aporia acraea* is one of several related species found in China.

Moths

The southern tropical forests are home to some impressively large moths, including the Atlas Moth (*Attacus atlas*), the world's largest. Its wings form a triangular shape and are intricately patterned in grey, brown and white. Rather similar is the almost equally large *Archaeoattacus edwardsii*. The moon moths (*Actias*) are also very fine tropical moths. They are pale green, but the hindwings have 10cm-long ribbon-like extensions that trail elegantly behind them as they fly. The owlet moth (*Nyctipao*) has dramatic eye-spots on the forewings, whose probable function is to startle bird predators.

The silkworm moth (*Bombyx mori*) is native to northern China. Although it is now common in cultivation, being the basis of the centuries-old silk industry, in fact it is rare in the wild. The caterpillars ('silkworms') are raised mainly on mulberry leaves, and the silk from their cocoons is harvested to make the fine thread from which silk items are spun.

The elegant atlas moth has the largest wing span of all moths.

THE SILK TRADE

Silkworms on mulberry leaves in Khotan on Silk Road.

The Chinese have been making silk for at least 3,000 years, and for much of that time the process was a well-guarded secret. Even when the material eventually became known in the West and was widely traded, the method of its manufacture lay shrouded in deep mystery. It was not until the Middle Ages that Europe eventually discovered how it was made. The Romans apparently came to believe that the Chinese made silk from the leaves of certain trees, but they eventually discovered the real process. At first silk cloth was restricted for use only by members of the Imperial family and other people of very high status, and it was also used for making a fine-grade paper. The high value of silk even led to its being used as a currency, and it was also used politically as a diplomatic gift. The regular trade in silk also gave its name to the famous Silk Roads that linked China and the West. Although mainly made from cocoons of the silk moth (*Bombyx mori*), various other moth species were also used, especially in Europe. The Chinese invented a machine that extracted the silk from the cocoons and wound the strands onto a spool, thus speeding the production process.

An active silk industry sprang up in Italy starting in the 11th and 12th centuries and came to be centred on Lucca, Florence, Genoa and Venice. Manufacture later developed in France and Britain as well. In the middle of the 19th century the European silk industry went into decline, partly due to diseases attacking both the caterpillars and the mulberry trees they fed on. In recent years, China has regained its position as the world's largest producer of silk.

BEETLES, BUGS, SPIDERS AND OTHERS

The Chinese relationship with invertebrates is complicated. Some are regarded as a nuisance or pests, while many are eaten – I have tasted stir-fried dragonfly larvae in Yunnan, where tropical wasp grubs are also a delicacy. Insect protein is very nutritious, it seems. Crickets are often kept for their 'singing' or for fighting sessions, and mole crickets (rare in Europe) are a frequent sight around street lamps at night in humid weather.

Beetles

By far the largest group of insects are the beetles (order Coleoptera). These outnumber all other animal groups, with an amazing total of at least 300,000 species, and with more and more being discovered and described, especially from the tropical forests. The evolutionary biologist Haldane, when asked by a clergyman what could be inferred about the mind of the Creator from a study of nature, famously replied: 'An inordinate fondness for beetles'. Unsurprisingly, China has an abundance of beetles, including many large and often colourful longhorned beetles, and bright shiny chrysomelids with metallic sheens. The five-horned rhinoceros beetle (*Eupatorus gracilicornis*) is a powerful insect, with five thorn-like projections on its head, and *Lucanus planeti* is a stag beetle, with antler-like forward-projecting horns. Another large beetle of tropical China is *Trictenotoma davidi*, one of a family of only 14 species. It is very large, up to 8cm, with a greenish body, large mandibles and fairly long antennae. It inhabits damp tropical forests, living mainly in or on the bark of trees.

Top Beetle with warning coloration feeding on *Arisaema* leaf.
Above A chafer beetle in Yunnan.

Bugs

Insects belonging to the order Hemiptera are the so-called 'true bugs'. They have piercing and sucking mouthparts, and come in a bewildering range of shapes and sizes. Some of the most bizarre are the colourful lantern bugs of the tropics (Fulgoridae). Some of these have strange lantern-like extensions to the head, thought to be important in mating displays, while others flash their wings to display disconcerting eye-spots to deter predators.

Cicadas are common in China, but are more often heard than seen, making their piercing calls from tree trunks and branches. Traditionally, many cicadas were caught and caged for the entertainment value of these 'songs', produced by rapid flexing of special membranes in the insect's cuticle. Cicadas were (and still are)

Stick insect moving over *Berberis*.

eaten in some parts of China, as are many other insects and their larvae. While most cicadas are grey-brown and inconspicuous, some of the tropical species are colourful. An example is the red-nosed cicada (*Scieroptera sanguinea*), which has dark wings and vivid red and black colours on its body, while others have green veined wings and bright red eyes.

Shield bugs have flat shiny bodies, often with bright colours. The tea seed bug (*Poecilocoris latus*) is orange, black and white, and is sometimes a pest in tea plantations, where large numbers may stunt the growth of the tea shrubs. Giant water bugs (Belastomatidae) are found in southern China. These large aquatic predators include tadpoles and even fish in their diet and catch their prey using their claw-like front legs. They are widely eaten, especially in Guangdong Province.

Stick and leaf insects

These insects, of the order Phasmatodea, are found mainly in the tropical south of China. The longest insect is the stick insect *Tirachidea westwoodi*, the female of which reaches 28cm, the male being a mere 18cm. Leaf insects (Phyllidae) are similar to stick insects, except that their bodies are laterally flattened to resemble leaves rather than twigs.

Grasshoppers and crickets

China has many grasshoppers and crickets (order Orthoptera), and crickets in particular play a large role in Chinese folklore and tradition. There is a long history of crickets being kept in special cages to entertain by their singing, in the manner of caged songbirds, a practice which still goes on today and involves many different species. Another large insect from the tropical south is the giant longhorned grasshopper. At 12cm, it can seem almost bird-like in flight. Mole-crickets (*Gryllotalpa*) are common in China and may sometimes be seen around street lights, to which they are attracted. Well-named, these chunky crickets have broad spade-like front claws that they use to construct underground burrows. Male mole-crickets even use burrows as amplifiers to broadcast their churring songs, which can be heard up to 1.5km away.

The orchid mantis disguises itself as an orchid flower. (FT)

Mantids

These impressive insects (order Mantodea) have triangular faces, huge compound eyes and fearsome front claws. Several species are found in China, especially in the south. A common mantis, brown with a green lateral stripe, is *Tenodera aridifolia*. One of the most interesting and unusual is the pure white orchid mantis (*Hymenopus*), which resembles a flower. Its legs even have petal-like flanges. It waits almost motionless, sometimes swaying gently as if in a breeze, and then strikes quickly when another insect strays too close. This amazing creature is a tropical species that just gets into China, in southernmost Yunnan. The slow movements interspersed with rapid attacking strikes of mantids are thought to have influenced some styles of traditional kung fu boxing.

Top Dragonfly at Mai Po Marshes, Hong Kong.
Above Nocturnal spider out hunting on wall.

Dragonflies and damselflies

These striking insects, of the order Odonata, dart over streams and lakes, and the nymphs of some species are so numerous in places that they are caught like fish and eaten lightly fried – a nutritious if somewhat unusual delicacy.

Spiders

Spiders belong to the class Arachnida, subclass Aranae. Large golden orb-web spiders of the genus *Nephila* can sometimes be spotted, especially in the tropical south, and they have the irritating habit of dangling at head height from trees and bushes, often over tracks.

Old World tarantulas are also found in the tropical regions, such as those in the genus *Haplopelma*. These can have legspans of up to 20cm and live in burrows up to several feet long, from which they emerge to capture insects and even small birds and rodents. They should not be handled as they can deliver a venomous bite. The golden earth tiger *H. huwenum* is found mainly in Guangxi Province, while the black earth tiger *H. haiwanum* is from Hainan.

Crustaceans

An interesting freshwater crustacean is the Chinese mitten crab (*Eriocheir sinensis*). A small crab, reaching some 8cm across, it has hairy, white-tipped claws, and is native to the rivers and estuaries of eastern China. In some places farmers raise mitten crabs in rice paddies. This crab is somewhat notorious outside China as it has become numerous and destructive to native wildlife in many other countries to which it has been exported, notably in Europe and North America.

Making
The Most Of It

Overlooking tropical rainforest on Hainan Island.

The raised walkway in Wild Elephant Valley, Xishuangbanna, allows visitors to watch elephants passing below.

Many visitors will gain the initial impression that China is distinctly unpromising as a wildlife-watching destination. There are a number of reasons for the apparent paucity of wildlife. Firstly, the main centres of population are for the most part concentrated in the eastern provinces and this is also where most of the industrial development has taken place. Secondly, the eastern lowlands, especially the lower reaches of the Yangtze and Yellow rivers, have long been used for the cultivation of rice and other crops, with most of the natural vegetation having been removed to make way for the agricultural expansion. Thirdly, the concept of conservation came late to China, and it is only in recent years that the country has begun to take seriously the preservation of natural habitats and their animals and plants. Fourthly, the Chinese have tended, with the exception of certain (mainly Buddhist) ethnic minorities, to regard nature as a storehouse to be plundered to satisfy human needs, rather than a valuable heritage to be protected in its own right. Yet there are some encouraging signs that this attitude is changing and many young Chinese people are now interested in green issues and in conservation, as indicated for example by the many active birding societies and clubs. Ecotourism from outside China has also snowballed and the Chinese government has not been slow to recognise the economic value of preserving nature.

A cable car ride gives an aerial view of South Sichuan Bamboo Sea.

Taking a boat ride in Yin Cui Gorge, Yunnan.

WHEN TO GO

In general, the best seasons for a visit to China are spring and autumn. Winters in the north and in the continental interior are very cold, and over much of central and southern China the summers can be muggy and also quite wet – an uncomfortable combination for the outdoor naturalist. The other factor determining the choice of season is the wildlife itself. If you are interested in migrant birds, then spring and autumn are the best times to visit, for example, the wetland reserves of the coastal regions. The spring migration is the busiest, and this gets under way as early as the beginning of April in the south, for example at Mai Po Marshes (Hong Kong). The autumn migration tends to be less concentrated and lasts from early August to early November, but this is also a rather unreliable period for weather, with storms and typhoons a possibility. For cranes and waterfowl at famous sites such as Beidaihe, Poyang Hu and Dongting Hu, winter is the best time to visit. In the temperate and subtropical forests, spring can be a magical time, as most of the birds will be in full song and breeding plumage, and butterflies and other insects will be emerging. For those whose main interest is the flora, the splendid alpine flowers of the highlands of Tibet, Sichuan and Yunnan will be at their best in early summer, while the subtropical and tropical areas will have much to offer throughout the year. The autumn colours of China's deciduous forests in the temperate central and northern regions are impressive and, if seeing this is your aim, then September and October are good months to choose.

Unless you have fluent Mandarin and an independent spirit it is best to go on an organised tour, and the range of these now on offer is amazing, with many tours specialising in wildlife, from dedicated birdwatching of the 'twitching' variety to more relaxed ecotours aimed at the generalist. A local guide is essential, preferably one with a good knowledge of the flora and fauna, though this can be hard to guarantee. Careful research online is seldom wasted effort and can make all the difference in finding the most suitable tour. In general, Chinese hotels are good value, and most are clean and welcoming to Western travellers, although prices are rising in tourist hotspots. Internal flights and trains are also relatively cheap, though the latter may be crowded and uncomfortable unless you book a soft sleeper.

It is a very good plan to avoid Chinese public holidays, as at these periods the internal tourism really takes off with people cramming into trains and planes and arriving at popular sites 'en masse'. Such 'honeypots' include Xiangshan Park (Fragrant Hills) near Beijing, Zhangjiajie in Hunan, and several popular sites in Sichuan, notably the panda breeding centre at Wolong (Sichuan), the holy mountain of Emei Shan and the beautiful World Heritage Sites of Huanglongsi and Jiuzhaigou. It is always possible to get away from the crowds by walking that little bit further from the main arrival point, but for wildlife watching it is usually better to visit at a quieter time if possible.

The richest regions for wildlife are southern and southwest China, especially the provinces of Sichuan and Yunnan, and these have been progressively well explored, becoming rather popular with tourists of all kinds. Less well known are the provinces of southeast China, and of these, Guangxi, Guangdong and Hunan are well worth

Top Looking into the heart of a *Primula* flower.
Above Using a hand lens to check out a *Cassiope* flower.

exploring. Tibet is huge and has fascinating wildlife and culture, but travel options are somewhat restricted and require more effort and planning.

WHAT TO TAKE

There are now many general travel guidebooks available on China, and it is a good idea to prepare for a visit by doing some serious background reading before you set off. Most will explain about the details of securing a visa, as well as offering useful phrases in Mandarin, and information about internal travel and accommodation. Some good recent guidebooks are included in the Further Reading section, as are suggested field guides for birds.

Clothes should be comfortable and lightweight, and fairly sturdy footwear will be necessary for upland and mountain regions. Remember that snakes can be a danger, particularly in the tropical and subtropical south, so footwear should not expose flesh. At high altitude and in the north it can get very cold, especially at night, even in summer, so warm clothing is usually essential. Lightweight rainproofs are also desirable, especially during the rainy season, roughly between May and September.

Binoculars are a must – ideally 8x40 or 10x50, and serious birders will also need a good telescope, especially at coastal sites.

Other essentials

Sunblock Apply thoroughly. At high altitudes, even though the air might be cool, the sun can burn you very quickly.

Insect repellent Use in the evenings and when walking, also spray over clothing.

Small rucksack Useful for carrying essentials such as a raincoat and spare plastic bags on day excursions.

Lightweight small towel Useful for padding camera gear and general drying.

Water bottle Keep filled with boiled and cooled water.

First-aid kit Essential for the travelling naturalist.

Toilet paper Toilets in the more basic hostels and restaurants, especially those that are off the beaten track, can be dreadful, so taking your own tissues is a sensible precaution.

HEALTH AND SAFETY

Consult travel guides and official websites and take proper medical advice when planning your trip. A few basic precautions are worth emphasising here.

- **Inoculations** The only requirement at the moment is yellow fever if coming from an area where this disease is endemic. But check with a doctor well before you travel.
- **Malaria** This is not a problem in most of China, but can occur in the tropical south. If travelling in that region it is wise to take preventative tablets (check with your doctor) and to take precautions to avoid being bitten.
- **Sunstroke and dehydration** Avoid direct exposure to the sun during the hottest part of the day, wear a hat and use sunscreen, and carry water. Note that in high-altitude areas, such as western Sichuan, northern Yunnan and Tibet, the sun can be very fierce and burning, even if the air feels cool.
- **Wild animals** Most wild animals avoid people, but a few are potentially dangerous and should be treated with respect. In tropical forests especially, it is always advisable to travel with a local guide.
- **Snakebite** Snakes are normally shy and move quickly away if disturbed. They rarely bite, but several poisonous snakes are found in China. Take simple precautions, like wearing closed shoes and watching where you put your hands and feet. In the event of a bite, get urgent medical help, but meanwhile lay the victim down, keep them still and calm and reassure them. An even-pressure bandage wrapped around the bitten limb (working upwards from the bite) helps inhibit the spread of venom. Never

The monocled cobra is highly poisonous.

apply a tourniquet, take aspirin or cut an incision. Note also that not every snakebite results in envenomation, and also bear in mind that the shock of being bitten – even by a harmless snake – can produce phantom symptoms. Try to identify the snake if possible (without further danger) as different snakes have different venoms, requiring different treatment.
- **Other bites and stings** Scorpions, some centipedes and spiders, and horseflies can deliver nasty bites, though few are dangerous. Wasp and bee stings can be very painful but seldom dangerous, unless you are allergic, in which case carry a special kit to prevent anaphylactic shock (again consult a doctor beforehand). After walking in long grass, check yourself for ticks.
- **Driving** China's ever-expanding road system is becoming more and more crowded as domestic car ownership increases, and there are also many lorries and buses to compete with. Roads outside of the main city areas are often still in a bad state, with pot-holes and cracks. Add to this a shocking accident rate, and the best advice is to avoid driving, but hire a good local driver if necessary.

Birdwatching in north Yunnan.

WATCHING FOR WILDLIFE

Botanists generally have it easier than naturalists whose main interest is in mammals or birds – at least the plants do not move around! For plants, it is simply a question of being in the right place at the right season (especially if seeing plants in flower is your objective), and then searching carefully in the right habitat.

For animals, different techniques come into play. Most wild mammals and birds in China are shy and wary of people, as indeed they tend to be elsewhere. Small wonder perhaps when you consider the decades of hunting and trapping they have endured. Exceptions might be birds of parks and gardens, which are often more approachable, as are some tropical forest species. Most woodland mammals are difficult to see in the wild – many are nocturnal, and nearly all are very timid. Monkeys will sometimes be quite prominent and will often stop and stare from a safe distance, for example on cliffs or rocky outcrops close to cover; macaques in particular are so used to begging from tourists at some sites that they have become a nuisance. Mammals of the open plains and grassland, or high rocky slopes, such as gazelles, Asiatic wild ass, and blue and Argali sheep, keep their distance, and much patience is required to get close to them. China's most famous mammals – giant panda, snow leopard, clouded leopard and tiger – are nearly impossible to see in the wild. The nearest you will get to these is in zoos or the panda breeding centre.

In the case of birds, finding interesting species is not so difficult. There are many fine wetlands where waders, wildfowl and cranes gather at predictable times, as well as a huge number of forest sites where fascinating birds can be seen in their natural habitats at almost any season. A telescope is useful at coastal sites for waders and wildfowl, but rather different techniques are required in woodland and forest. In general, birds are most active early in the morning and tend to be less easy to find around the middle of the day, although they usually become more noticeable again in the late afternoon. The importance of learning bird calls and songs cannot be over-emphasised. This is especially true in woodland, particularly in subtropical and tropical forests where it is often quite hard to spot the individual birds. Most birds have very distinctive calls, which, with practice, can be used in identification. Some birds will reply to an imitation of their call and may then approach you, offering a better view. The best advice is to go with a local expert and concentrate on learning some of the commonest calls and songs; this will certainly add to your enjoyment of, for example, a ramble in the lush rainforests of the south. Forest birds are usually best watched at the edge of the forest, or at a clearing or stream. Fruiting trees sometimes act as magnets for certain forest birds, so these are worth watching out for. Wait for the birds to come to you rather than trying to stalk them down. When birding in humid forests in the south, it is a good plan to spray your socks and boots with insecticide to deter leeches, which can be troublesome in some areas.

PHOTOGRAPHING NATURAL CHINA
(by Heather Angel)

China has a varied climate, covering a huge latitude range with diverse habitat types that support a rich assortment of plant and animal species. The potential for wildlife photography in China would therefore seem to be huge. However, due to habitat loss and the tradition of capturing an astonishing range of wildlife as food, much of China's wildlife is thinly spread and under threat. Apart from concentrations of breeding and wintering wetland and coastal birds, it takes considerable effort to find many animals.

Nonetheless, with increased awareness of the need for habitat protection, the number of nature reserves in China continues to increase. This means that finding opportunities for wildlife photography is becoming easier.

China has some stunning and unique landscapes embracing spectacular mountain scenery, the travertine terraces at Huanglong, Baishui and within Jiuxiang cave, intense blue lakes and travertine terraces at Jiuzhaigou, geological formations referred to as stone forests or 'Shilin' most famously in Yunnan but also at Wansheng in Sichuan, and extensive bamboo forests in Anhui and Sichuan. The only snag is that the best scenic spots are invariably a magnet to Chinese tourists, who pose in front of the best viewpoints! The solution is to get there early in the day.

As in Japan, Chinese camera enthusiasts will know the best place and time to photograph sunrise or sunset at any time of year. They will also be

Backlit bamboo leaves look dramatic against an unlit backdrop, South Sichuan Bamboo Sea.

145

naturally curious about your equipment and keen to check out the make and model of your camera.

In addition to the giant panda, notable Chinese wildlife includes the more widespread red panda, several species of snub-nosed and tropical monkeys, a galaxy of striking pheasants long prized in Western aviaries, the green peafowl and the largest amphibian in the world.

China's iconic giant panda lives in remote mountainous terrain where researchers can take days, or even weeks, to track one down. However, at the giant panda breeding centre at Wolong in Sichuan Province, pandas can be photographed within natural vegetation.

Isolated pine trees on Huangshan (Yellow Mountain) in Anhui Province make striking silhouettes against a colourful dawn sky.

Much information about Chinese reserves can be found on the internet, although not all sites are in English. Chinese travel agents run eco tours, as do Western wildlife tour companies.

Now that travel for overseas visitors to China is so much easier, it is also quite possible to devise your own tailor-made tour to the wilder parts of China, preferably after you have experienced this vast country with a group tour. You will need to know where to go and what to see, so make sure you ask all the right questions beforehand to establish you have allowed enough time to get from A to B. Typically, drivers know the times local sites near their home town but since they rarely travel far afield, travel times over long distances are a guesstimate and are often underestimated.

Top An upright format is best for taking tall flower spikes such as this *Meconopsis prattii* at Napa Hai in Yunnan.
Above An overhead shot of a ladybird on an open *Potentilla* flower is simplified with an out-of-focus background.

You should produce a printout of your itinerary so an English-speaking guide can brief the driver; otherwise you could easily end up at a tourist trap or visiting a series of temples. Within China, the checked baggage allowance is only 20kg, so you need to pack well below the international airline allowance to allow for collecting leaflets, or buying books with pictures of scenic parts of China.

Whenever I visit a new part of China, one of my first ports of call is the botanic garden within any major city. This is a good opportunity to get to know regional plants. Also, wild birds are generally more approachable here since they have become habituated not only to people but also the loud 'muzak' of the early morning *tai chi* sessions!

EQUIPMENT

Standard point and shoot digital cameras are now available with lenses up to x12 optical zoom. With such a lens, habitat shots and close-ups of flowers and larger approachable wildlife can be taken. Many of these cameras also have inbuilt image stabilisers (IS) which enable the camera to be handheld at slower shutter speeds without the risk of camera shake. However, for the enthusiast, a digital single lens reflex (D-SLR) camera with a selection of lenses is the most versatile set-up for photographing wildlife. The choice of lenses will depend on what subjects are to be photographed. A good lens for habitats is a wide-angle to short telephoto – something in the region of 24–120mm.

Birds and mammals, on the other hand, will need much longer lenses – at least 300mm, preferably more, but a 100–300mm zoom is a good starting point. Buying a long lens with an inbuilt image stabiliser or vibration reduction (VR) system will make it possible to take handheld shots in low light levels. A true macro lens, designed to be used at close range, is a must for taking close-ups of flowers and insects.

The advantage of working with any digital camera is that the ISO (sensitivity to light) can be changed frame by frame. The downside is that camera batteries, as well as downloaders and external hard drives, have to be recharged. China has two types of plugs: a two-pin round plug and an angled two-pin (like Australia), so it is essential to take at least one, maybe two, international adaptors. On any trip, images should be backed up by downloading from memory cards onto a laptop, a downloader or a portable hard drive. A hard drive with a good screen, which allows images to be viewed and edited, is useful, but it will need recharging more frequently than one which does not have a viewing window.

Changing lenses on digital cameras increases the chance of dust particles being attracted to the sensor. In remote locations there is no chance of walking into a dealer to get it cleaned, but this is now a very easy job with a sensor cleaning brush, known as the Arctic Butterfly. A small motor powered by two AAA batteries spins the brush to put an electrical charge on the bristles which then attract dust. By locking up the mirror, the brush can be gently stroked across the sensor.

Carrying a tripod can be tiresome, but it does make working in poor light feasible. An alternative camera support is a monopod which is more flexible for working with moving animals.

TECHNIQUE
When taking habitat shots try to include some foreground interest. Avoid a large area of drab, overcast, or cloudless sky – either crop it out or break it up with a tree or mountain peak – and avoid getting distracting objects in the foreground or background. It is all too easy to focus attention on the subject without scanning the frame for eyesores, so it pays to check the background before releasing the shutter. Using a shallow depth of field to blur the background can also help, or you can simply reframe the shot to crop out eyesores. If there are distracting branches cutting across the subject, often simply changing the camera position by moving to one side will be enough to gain a clear viewpoint. Look out for dramatic lighting, such as the papery flaking bark of birches lit from behind, which will glow within the landscape.

A zoom telephoto lens was ideal for this tight crop on a green peacock's iridescent tail feathers.

A simple way to photograph close-ups of flowers is either to use the macro mode on a short telephoto lens, or attach a close-up lens to the front of a prime lens. But if you want to concentrate on close-ups of flowers as well as insects, a 90mm or 105mm macro lens is ideal. A small reflector (which can be carried on a photopack using a carabiner) will help to boost low light on plants. Even a piece of silver cooking foil wrapped around a notebook or piece of card can help. Gardening kneepads ease the discomfort of kneeling on hard ground for low-level shots of flowers.

Inside an evergreen forest little light penetrates, so here a tripod is obligatory for habitat shots and plant portraits. A flash is also useful for taking moving subjects inside any forest. Fill flash – where the daylight exposure is taken and the flash is underexposed by 1.3–1.7 stops – can add a catchlight to a dark eye set within the black eye patches on panda faces or within black feathers of birds. You can get away with using a slower shutter speed if you pan the camera and follow a bird in flight or a running mammal.

Try to vary shots by taking both horizontal and vertical compositions. If an animal accepts you and does not flee, stay to get some behavioural shots as well as straight portraits. Eye-to-eye portraits of animals looking straight at the camera immediately arrest attention, while cute baby animals never fail to appeal.

Fish can be taken in public aquaria and zoos, but it is sensible not to visit on a Sunday when they are very crowded with families who love to sit their child on the base of the window for a picture with the fish behind! When photographing fish or plants down through the water surface, a polarising filter is useful for eliminating the reflection of the sky.

Holy mountains such as Emei Shan in Sichuan have a vast number of steps – with shallow risers – leading up and down the mountain. It can be quite wearing walking up and down them carrying full camera gear, so a sensible option is to take a cable car. Fortunately, virtually all mountainous scenic spots in China have a cable car to access the mountains. Failing that, it does not cost much to hire a porter. While riding in cable cars, overviews can be taken of the terrain below if it is not enveloped in low cloud.

Many local and national reserves have been set up for individual species, including several for the giant panda – Wolong being the flagship one. Within this rich bio-diverse habitat many other species of animal and plant also benefit from being protected.

Photographing wildlife is always something of a lottery. However exhaustive the research and planning, there is no guarantee that the animals will turn up or behave as you predict, that a storm won't flatten the flowers or that the weather will be conducive to photography. But with digital cameras, shots no longer have to be rationed and it is possible to experiment with using different combinations of shutter speed and aperture, as well as different compositions. Frames which did not work can be edited out. It is even possible to crop images later on the computer, although the aim should be to strive for perfect in-camera composition.

Eye-to-eye portraits such as this red panda give more impact than when an animal is taken side on.

CHECKLIST FOR DIGITAL SLR CAMERAS

- Camera body
- Lenses
- Polarising filter
- Tripod (or monopod)
- Reflector for plants
- Flash
- Charger for camera battery
- Spare batteries for flash
- Laptop or external hard drive
- CDs if taking laptop
- Charger for external hard drive
- Sensor cleaner
- Field notebook
- Plug adaptors
- Gardening kneepads
- Arctic Butterfly sensor cleaning brush

A low camera angle with a tight crop gives a fresh angle on a giant panda. Notice how a catchlight reveals the position of the black eye within the black eye patch.

Photographing travertine terraces at Huanglong.

WHERE TO GO

Weathered limestone peaks in Stone Forest
National Geopark, Yunnan Province.

CONSERVATION AND NATURE RESERVES

China now has a large number of protected areas, designated in a somewhat bewildering array of categories, including the following:

- Ecological Function Reserves
- Forest Parks (FP)
- Marine Special Reserves
- National Geological Parks
- Nature Reserves (NR)
- Public Parks
- Scenic Landscape and Historical Sites
- Thematic Gardens
- Urban Wetland Parks
- Water Conservation Scenic Parks
- Wetland Parks

The followings terms and abbrevations are also useful to know:
WHS: World Heritage Site
MAB: Man and Biosphere Reserve
RAMSAR: Internationally important wetland

Conservation is now heading towards the top of China's political agenda, and not before time, as nature has for far too long been over-exploited for food and to make way for the headlong rush to industrialise.

In recent years, the number of reserves in the country has increased rapidly. The first nature reserve was established in 1956. By 1978, there were still only 34, but since then the number has risen dramatically – more than 600 by 1990, more than 925 by 1997, 1,276 by 2001, and 1,551 by the end of 2003. If we include all protected areas, not just strict reserves, by the end of 2005 China had established more than 5,000 such areas, representing about 18% of the land area – an impressive total indeed. By the same date, the total number of nature reserves reached 2,349, covering some 15% of the land. By 2004, 26 of the reserves were designated as World Biosphere Reserves by UNESCO. By 2005, 30 nature reserves had been designated as important wetland sites by RAMSAR, and by 2006 there were 33 World Heritage Sites.

In addition to nature reserves, there are also 1,400 Forest Parks, 800 Scenic Landscape and Historical Sites, about 140 National Geological Parks, some 50 Water Conservation Scenic Parks and more than 1,000 small nature reserves. Although these are diverse and administered in different ways and for different purposes, all qualify as protected areas and therefore together all help to conserve and showcase China's wildlife.

In the highly populated south and east, the reserves are numerous, though mostly small, contrasting with the smaller number of mostly very large reserves in the relatively sparsely populated west. The largest of all, Qiangtang Nature Reserve, protects a massive chunk of Tibet the size of the whole of Italy! More than 70% of China's nature reserves are managed by the State Forestry Administration, and altogether more than ten agencies are involved in nature reserve management.

Although this looks impressive, in fact the protected areas vary in the degree to which the wildlife is actually preserved, with illegal hunting and other exploitation remaining a problem in many cases. As in many parts of the world, there are issues of conflict between the needs of the local people (who are often poor) and the reserves, and illegal logging, hunting and plant collecting are widespread. But efforts are being made to reconcile traditional use by locals with nature conservation. Further problems arise from the ways in which China's reserves are administered. Management is often rather patchy, with poorly trained staff and inadequate budgets – as in the case of the provinces of Xinjiang, Qinghai, Gansu and Inner Mongolia in the north, and Yunnan, Guangxi and Guangdong in the south.

REGIONS AND SITES

As China is such a vast country with complicated topography and wide variations of climate and altitude, it is hard to define distinct bio-geographical regions. Therefore, in order to guide the reader to a representative variety of China's habitats and special species we have divided the country into eight 'eco-regions', defined largely on the basis of topography and climate. Be aware that these are to some extent arbitrary, and that species and habitats will naturally overlap. Within each of these regions we have selected representative and interesting sites, many (but not all) of which are nature reserves.

Pitiao River in Wolong NR after an overnight snowfall.

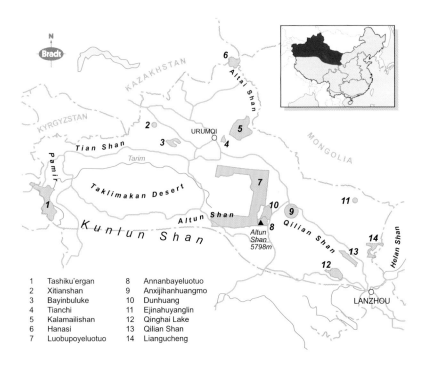

1	Tashiku'ergan	8	Annanbayeluotuo
2	Xitianshan	9	Anxijihanhuangmo
3	Bayinbuluke	10	Dunhuang
4	Tianchi	11	Ejinahuyanglin
5	Kalamailishan	12	Qinghai Lake
6	Hanasi	13	Qilian Shan
7	Luobupoyeluotuo	14	Liangucheng

1. DESERT REGION OF NORTHWEST CHINA (14 SITES)

This is a large region, dominated by deserts and semi-deserts and surrounded by mountain ranges: the Altai Shan in the north; Tian Shan in the northwest; Pamir in the west; Kunlun, Altun and Qilian Shan in the south and Helan Shan in the southeast. In the last-named range, grassland communities occupy much of the lower slopes, with Siberian elm (*Ulmus pumila*) near the streams, scrub with rose and juniper, and stands of red pine (*Pinus tabulaeformis*) in dry sites. At higher levels there are forests of spruce, birch and poplar. Qilian Shan in northern Qinghai rises to 5,547m and forms the northeast rim of the Tibetan Plateau. Coniferous forests on the northern side have spruce, fir and juniper. Mammals of the area include snow leopard, white-lipped deer, wild yak, Tibetan antelope and ibex. The montane forests feature Siberian fir and Siberian larch in the Altai Shan and mainly Schrenk spruce (*Picea schrenkiana*) in the Tian Shan.

Southern Xinjiang contains the vast Taklimakan Desert, which covers about 742,000km² between the Kunlun and Tian Shan ranges. China's largest desert, it features mobile sands with very sparse vegetation and low biodiversity. The Tarim Basin here once had forests of poplar alongside the Tarim River and tributaries, but most have long gone, although poplars are often planted as windbreaks. This has the distinction of being the driest place in China, and is best visited during the summer.

Native mammals include Bactrian camel and Asiatic wild ass. Evaporation has created salt lakes and deposits, although there is also fresh water associated with springs and oases fed by mountain snowmelt. Permanent water has allowed some woodland to become established, mainly dominated by poplars, although most has been destroyed. The desert experiences extreme variations in temperature – the winter–summer range may be 30°C, and day–night 20°C. Annual precipitation is less than 10mm in the driest areas, but is generally higher towards the fringing mountains. Where present, the plant life features drought-resistant species such as tamarisk, *Alhagi sparsifolia, Ephedra przewalskii, Haloxylon* spp., *Karelinia caspica, Nitraria sphaerocarpus* and *Scorzonera divaricata.*

In this region many birds, such as bee-eater, capercaillie, fieldfare, little bittern and great grey and red-backed shrikes, are at the eastern limit of their range, but the birding is spiced by endemic species including Mongolian and Xinjiang ground jays and blue-capped redstart. Raven, great and (occasionally) houbara bustards (*Chlamydotis undulata*), steppe eagle, long-legged buzzard (*Buteo rufinus*), black-bellied sandgrouse (*Pterocles orientalis*), hoopoe and both desert and isabelline wheatears may be spotted in the vast plains.

Tashiku'ergan NR (Xinjiang) is a large reserve on the far western border of the province, covering 15,000km² and ranging from 3,000–8,311m. The main habitats here are arid desert, cold highland scrub and alpine meadows, with occasional stands of poplar, willow and wild rose. Notable mammals include snow leopard, Argali sheep, ibex, marmot, brown bear, wolf and fox.

Snow leopards are found on higher ground in northwest China's deserts.

West Tian Shan (Xitianshan) NR (Xinjiang) is a much smaller reserve in the north, protecting part of the impressive Tian Shan range. The vegetation here ranges, with increasing altitude, from arid steppe to spruce forest and finally to alpine habitats and glaciers. Snow leopards may still lurk on the rocky slopes. Most of the ridges are about 4,000m and some reach 7,400m, the highest being 7,435m. Forests of Schrenk spruce clothe some of the slopes, and stone marten (*Martes foina*), Argali sheep, ibex, black stork and golden eagle inhabit the reserve. Other trees of the Tian Shan include the local mountain ash (*Sorbus tianschanica*), willows and birches. The highest habitats have alpine meadows of sedge with dwarf birch, and between about 1,000 and 1,700m there are interesting deciduous forests containing wild relatives of apple (*Malus sieversii*) and apricot (*Prunus armeniaca*).

To the southeast lies **Bayinbuluke NR** (Xinjiang), dominated mainly by lower-altitude mountains between 2,500 and 2,800m, and covering some 1,487km², with grassland, mountains and lakes. This is another haunt of snow leopard and Argali sheep, and whooper swans famously gather at the lakes. The raptors are of interest, with golden eagle and Pallas's fish eagle (*Haliaeetus leucoryphus*).

Tianchi NR (Xinjiang), the magnificent West Heaven Lake, one of China's tourist highlights, is set in stunning scenery, surrounded by steep wooded hills, and is a popular summer destination. The lake, about 105m deep, is some 110km east of Urumqi and lies at 2,000m. Notable species are *Picea schrenkiana*, poplars, mountain ash and wild rose.

Tianchi or Heavenly Lake is backed by the snow-capped Tian Shan range.

Kalamailishan NR (Xinjiang), to the east of Tianchi, is a large reserve of 18,000km², featuring mainly arid, desert habitats, with saxaul (*Haloxylon*) prominent. It lies at an altitude of between 800 and 1,472m. This rather forbidding country is home to great bustard, Argali sheep, goitered gazelle and Asiatic wild ass. Przewalski's horse is also now being reintroduced in this reserve.

Tucked away in the far north of the province, on the edge of the Altai Mountains where China meets Mongolia, Russia and Kazakhstan, **Hanasi NR (Kanas Lake)** (Xinjiang) has dense conifer forests dominated by Siberian spruce (*Picea obovata*) and Siberian larch (*Larix sibirica*), with alpine meadows above. The altitude ranges from 1,300–4,300m and, in addition to the lake, the main habitats are grassland, coniferous forests, mountain peaks and glaciers. The birds and mammals include pine bunting (*Emberiza leucocephalos*), ortolan (*Emberiza hortunala*), crossbill, black kite, goosander, goldeneye (*Bucephala clangula*), black stork, black grouse, golden eagle, ibex, brown bear, lynx, Pallas's cat, blue and Argali sheep, moose and red deer.

Luobupoyeluotuo NR (Xinjiang), the Lop Nur Wild Camel NR, is very large, covering 78,000km², and is dominated by arid sandy desert with very sparse vegetation. Set up especially for the wild Bactrian camel, the reserve also has snow leopard, lynx, wolf, brown bear and Argali sheep.

Not far from each other in the northwest of Gansu Province, towards the east of the vast Taklamakan Desert, are the desert reserves of **Annanbayeluotuo NR** and

Hanasi NR is a place to see moose.

Anxijihanhuangmo NR (Anxi Dry Desert). Both have the local poplar (*Populus euphratica*) and drought-tolerant plants such as saxaul. Bactrian camel, snow leopard, lynx, Argali and blue sheep and Tibetan snowcock can be found in the former. Between these is **Dunhuang NR** featuring huge rolling sand dunes, some nearly 300m high. Vegetation is sparse and animal life restricted to specialised species such as sand geckos and agamid lizards. The nearby oasis is fertile, with stands of poplars, often planted here as windbreaks.

Look out for black storks at upland lakes. (MW)

Ejinahuyanglin NR (Inner Mongolia), right in the northeast of the province, has Gobi Desert ecosystems with scattered Euphrates poplar (*Populus euphratica*) forests. The rare relict gull (*Larus relictus*) breeds in this area.

Qinghai Lake (Koko Nor) (Qinghai) is a huge, rather saline lake lying in the southeast of this region, at about 3,200m. It is surrounded by rolling hills with cold temperate meadow vegetation, featuring sedges. This lake is very important as a breeding site for several interesting birds, including brown-headed and Pallas's gulls, cormorant, avocet (*Recurvirostra avosetta*), bar-headed goose and black-necked crane. Mongolian ground-jay is another interesting local bird. The burrowing black-lipped pika is a fairly common small mammal, while goitered gazelle can be seen grazing, as can Przewalski's gazelle, the world's most endangered ungulate.

Qilian Shan (Qinghai) is a mountain range in the northeast of the Tibetan Plateau, with the desert to the north. Subalpine conifer forests and meadows give way to scrub above about 3,300m and this to alpine cushion-plant habitats above 4,500m. Notable species are snow leopard, Asiatic wild ass, marmot, white-lipped deer, Argali sheep, eastern imperial eagle (*Aquila heliaca*)

Whooper swans can tolerate icy water.

and both blue eared-pheasant and blood pheasant. To the east, at lower altitude, lies **Liangucheng** (Gansu), a reserve featuring plains and hills with desert vegetation. Mammals here include Chinese mountain cat and goitered gazelle, and this is a good spot for eagles and other birds of prey.

Asiatic or Tibetan wild ass can form large herds.

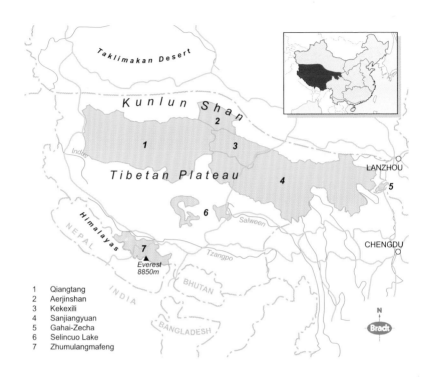

1 Qiangtang
2 Aerjinshan
3 Kekexili
4 Sanjiangyuan
5 Gahai-Zecha
6 Selincuo Lake
7 Zhumulangmafeng

2. HIGH PLATEAU REGION OF WEST CHINA (7 SITES)

The gigantic Tibetan Plateau, the largest, highest and youngest mountain plateau in the world, dominates most of western China. Centred on Tibet (Xizang), it also occupies much of neighbouring Qinghai and extends into southern Xinjiang and northwest Sichuan. At 2.5 million km² it accounts for a quarter of the whole of China, yet has less than 1% of the population and less than 1% of cultivated land. Here the average altitude is 4,500m. Rainfall is low, the annual total in the range of

Bar-headed geese migrate over the Himalayas. (GG)

100–300mm, falling mainly as erratic storms. Although moist monsoon air wells up from the south in summer, the massive Himalayas are an effective barrier, so by the time this air reaches Tibet it has lost most of its water. In winter, the temperature often dips to -40°C.

The native wildlife is adapted to the arid, cold, high-altitude conditions: characteristic mammals include yak, Asiatic wild ass, chiru, Argali and blue sheep and snow leopard, and wolves are not uncommon, preying on marmots, pikas

162

and other animals. Tibetan snowcock is a typical bird of the region, several large lakes are home to Pallas's gulls, bar-headed geese and black-necked cranes, and the strange and elusive ibisbill occurs along some rivers. Lammergeiers and Himalayan griffon vultures are typical scavengers of this region, and golden eagles are not uncommon. Smaller birds include Guldenstadt's redstart and various rosefinches.

Over much of the plateau the climate is too cold and dry and the soil too thin to support much vegetation, and cushion plants and hardy grasses dominate. Variations in moisture result in either meadow steppe or more sparse alpine communities. There are some isolated pockets of woodland in valleys on the plateau, with willow, juniper and shrubby tamarisks. But it is only in the river valleys and foothills of the extreme southeast that the conditions really favour woodland and forest, and here the flora includes many beautiful alpine flowers. This is also

The Himalayan tahr is related to wild goats.

the centre of distribution for rhododendron species. Feathergrasses are typical in the steppe habitats, although the grassland here is often patchy, with sedges dominant in colder sites. Alpine cushion plants include edelweiss (*Leontopodium*) and hardy shrubs such as *Potentilla fruticosa*. Parts of the plateau, especially in the east and south (the moister regions), are a botanist's paradise, with many alpine favourites such as gentians, saxifrages, primulas and rhododendrons.

Qiangtang (Chang Tang) NNR (Tibet). This huge area in the northwest of the Tibetan Plateau covers 300,000km² of steppe and alpine habitats at 4,300m and higher. The wild mammals include chiru, Tibetan gazelle, Argali and blue sheep, wild yak, Asiatic wild ass, snow leopard, brown bear, wolf and lynx. The chiru in particular is threatened by slaughter for its fine wool, smuggled to India and used for shahtoosh shawls. Other mammals here are black-lipped pika, Tibetan (*Vulpes ferrilata*) and red foxes, Himalayan marmot and Tibetan woolly hare. White-lipped deer, endemic to the Tibetan Plateau, can be found in the eastern section. The dominant vegetation is sparse steppe grassland featuring purple feathergrass (*Stipa purpurea*), with sedges such as *Carex moorcroftii* and cushion plants and alpines including *Leontopodium, Saussurea, Arenaria bryophylla* and *Thylacospermum caespitosum*. At lower altitudes, legumes such as *Astragalus* and *Oxytropis* feature, along with shrubs such as *Potentilla fructicosa*.

Aerjinshan NNR (Xinjiang) is another reserve of high-plateau habitats, in the deep southeast of the province in the Altun Mountains which form part of the northern rim of the Tibetan Plateau. Adjacent, to the south, is **Kekexili** (Qinghai), another large reserve with extensive alpine grasslands and meadows.

Sanjiangyuan NNR (Qinghai) is a huge reserve in southern Qinghai, which covers the headwaters of the three major rivers – Yellow, Yangtze and Lancang (Mekong), protecting high-altitude habitats, including wetlands, for chiru, yak, Asiatic wild ass and black-necked crane, among others. **Gahai-Zecha NR** (Qinghai), to the east, at the Gansu border, has high mountain grassland, shrub and forests, with some wetlands. Other birds include golden eagle and Pallas's fish eagle, black vulture (*Aegypius monachus*) and Sichuan jay (*Perisoreus internigrans*).

The scenic north route from Lhasa to Shigatze in Tibet (GPK)

Selincuo Lake NR (Tibet's second largest lake) lies in the centre of the Tibetan Plateau, between 4,000m and 6,000m, and this reserve holds some of the main breeding sites for the rare black-necked crane, whose main habitats are high-altitude steppe and marshy wetlands. There is a large resident population of chiru around the lake and also a large colony of Pallas's gulls on an island on Tsoe Lake.

Zhumulangmafeng NR MAB (Tibet), also known as Zhufeng, protects almost 34,000km^2 of high plateau and mountains, rising to the 8,848m peak of Everest (Zhumulangma) on the Nepalese border. This is classic snow leopard country, and the area also has Assamese macaque and Himalayan tahr. As well as protecting high-altitude wildlife on her flanks, this, the world's tallest peak, is sacred to the Tibetans and regarded as the Mother Goddess of the World.

1	Liupanshan	9	Nanwenghe	17	Dongwandashan
2	Baijitan	10	Humahe	18	Xingkaihu
3	Helan Shan	11	Zhalong	19	Jingbo Lake
4	Xi'erduosi	12	Momoge	20	Hunchun
5	Xilin Gele	13	Xianghai	21	Changbaishan
6	Dalaihu	14	Keerxin	22	Dalian Banhaibao
7	Hanma	15	Sanjiang	23	Shedao-Laotieshan
8	Huzhong	16	Honghe		

3. MOUNTAIN, FOREST AND GRASSLAND REGION OF NORTH CHINA (23 SITES)

This region consists of the plains of the northeast with their surrounding mountain ranges (Hinggan and Changbai). The climate is affected by the adjacent mass of Asia and is continental, with long, cold and rather dry winters. The summers, by contrast, are rainy. In some areas the plains feature swamps and small lakes with reedbeds. In the far north the taiga forests are dominated by coniferous trees, but further south the mountains show marked altitudinal zonation of vegetation, with a range of habitats. Changbai Shan, for example, has rich broadleaf deciduous forests, swamps, mixed conifer and broadleaf communities, pure conifer forests and alpine tundra.

The broadleaf trees include Mongolian oak (*Quercus mongolica*), Amur lime (*Tilia amurensis*), ash (*Fraxinus mandschurica*) and the birch *Betula ermanii*. Notable amongst the conifers are Korean pine, the fir *Abies holophylla*, red pine (*Pinus densiflora*) and Japanese yew (*Taxus cuspidata*). The famous ginseng grows in the herb layer of these forests, as does Manchurian ginger (*Asarum heterotropoides*) and the orchid *Gastrodia*. The orchid in particular, a medicinal plant, has suffered badly from over-collection, as has ginseng, which has become extinct over much of its former range.

In the Da Hinggan Mountains Daurian larch (*Larix dahurica*) is a dominant tree above about 500m, along with Mongolian oak.

The habitats of this region are rather mixed, with extensive swamps and lakes occupying many of the broad valleys. Typical mammals are sable (*Martes zibellina*), wolverine (*Gulo gulo*), arctic hare (*Lepus arcticus*), moose, red, sika and roe deer, Siberian musk deer (*Moschus moschiferus*), brown and Asiatic black bears and the rare Amur (Siberian) tiger and leopard. Hazel grouse is a characteristic bird of these northern forests, while cranes and storks breed in the marshes. Some of the wetlands are important as breeding grounds for red-crowned crane and Saunders's gull.

The gently rolling temperate steppe grasslands extend mainly southwest from the Da Hinggan Mountains, on the Nei Mongol Plateau, and gradually grade into the deserts to the far west. The grasses include the attractive feather grasses (*Stipa* spp.) with their delicate flowers.

Liupanshan (Ningxia) is right in the centre of China, in the hills of southern Ningxia. This reserve has a good mixture of habitats – upland grassland and steppe, with temperate deciduous broad-leaved and mixed coniferous forests. Pallas's fish eagle is known in this area. **Baijitan** (Ningxia) in the far north of the province features hilly country on the edge of the desert, with scattered forest, while **Helan Shan** (Ningxia/Inner Mongolia), further to the north, has splendid mountain forests protecting the Qinghai spruce (*Picea crassifolia*). This is also a site for the blue eared-pheasant, black stork and lesser kestrel (*Falco naumanni*) as well as blue sheep. Close by, **Xi'erduosi NR** (Inner Mongolia) is set in the transition zone from grassland to desert, and features freshwater and saline pools. This is a breeding site for the rare relict gull.

Right at the centre of Inner Mongolia lies China's first steppe grassland reserve, **Xilin Gele NR MAB**, a large reserve of more than 10,775km². About 600km north of Beijing, this site also protects some sandy wetlands. Steppe grasses include feathergrasses (*Stipa* spp.), and there is also scattered woodland of poplar, birch and spruce, and some herds of Mongolian gazelle.

Dalaihu NR MAB (Inner Mongolia), further north, is another fine reserve. The habitats include river, marsh, scrub and reedbeds, as well as China's fourth largest lake, set in a general landscape of feathergrass-dominated steppe. The brackish waters support rare birds, including Baikal teal, Oriental stork, Siberian, white-naped and red-crowned cranes, great bustard and relict gull, and Mongolian gazelle occurs too.

Top A frosty-faced Amur tiger at first light.
Above Pair of red-crowned cranes.

Wolverine walking over snow.

In the far northeast of China, where the narrow western arm of Heilongjiang arches over northern Inner Mongolia, there is a cluster of important reserves protecting the northern forests, dominated mainly by Siberian flora and fauna. **Hanma NR** (Inner Mongolia) and **Huzhong NR** (Heilongjiang) lie adjacent, and both have fine taiga coniferous forest clothing their hills, with northern species such as moose, wolverine and hazel grouse. Red-crowned, Siberian and white-naped cranes and scaly-sided merganser may be seen in this area. A little to the east is **Nanwenghe NR** (Heilongjiang) with ancient taiga and also wet meadows. These forests of pine, spruce and larch also have the interesting Amur corktree (*Phellodendron amurense*). This is a good spot for wetland birds, including swan goose and hooded crane. The northernmost of all our selected sites is **Humahe NR** (Heilongjiang) occupying a splendid mountain valley in this remote region. The wetlands here have Oriental stork, Baikal teal and scaly-sided merganser.

In southwest Heilongjiang, the marshes, lakes and reedbeds of **Zhalong NR** offer a breeding ground for rare red-crowned, white-naped, Siberian and demoiselle cranes, with common and hooded cranes also passing through. Other wetland birds include swans, cormorant, herons, bitterns, spoonbills, white (*Ciconia ciconia*) and black storks, black-headed ibis (*Threskiornis melanocephalus*) and many species of duck including scaly-sided merganser and mandarin. Siberian roe deer (*Capreolus pygargus*), badger (*Meles meles*) and red fox breed here and Mongolian gazelle can sometimes be seen on the grassy plains nearby. Amphibians are in abundance, with tree frogs, the Mongolian toad, black-spotted frog and the rare frog *Rana amurensis*. Nearby **Momoge NR** (Jilin) has similar habitats and wildlife, with great bustard possible on the grassland.

Xianghai NR (Jilin) and the adjacent reserve of **Keerxin** (Inner Mongolia) feature sparse forest (with anti-desertification plantations) and scrub in a semi-arid region, with wetlands. Lesser kestrel, cranes, swan goose and great bustard can be seen here.

Right on the far northeastern border, where the Amur River swings north into Russia, lies **Sanjiang NR** (Heilongjiang), with its important high-altitude wetlands – a mix of rivers, bogs and flooded meadows. This is another vital reserve for cranes (white-naped and red-crowned) as well as Oriental stork, swan goose and scaly-sided merganser. Another wetland reserve close by is **Honghe NR**, a marshy area with varied wetlands and excellent wetland birds. This is the main breeding site for Oriental stork, and also features black stork, cranes, whooper swan and mandarin duck.

Dongwandashan, in the east of Heilongjiang near the Russian border, is a refuge for the Amur tiger, and has fine original coniferous forest. Nearby **Xingkaihu NR** (Xingkai Lake) has good populations of wetland birds, with cranes, Chinese egret, tundra and whooper swans and several duck species including Baer's pochard, as does **Jingbo Lake** (Heilongjiang) near the border with Jilin. This reserve covers 1,260km² and rises to about 1,400m. The vegetation includes mixed forests of conifers (Korean pine and *Larix* spp.) and deciduous broadleaved trees (*Acer* spp. and *Quercus* spp.). The volcanic lake is very scenic and surrounded by forested hillsides. Amur tigers occasionally visit, and other mammals include lynx, musk, red and sika deer, wild boar, Chinese goral and Siberian chipmunk.

Hunchun NNR (Jilin) near the border with North Korea and Russia is one of the strongholds of the rare Amur tiger that breeds here in a region dominated by original coniferous forests. Further south lies **Changbaishan NR MAB** (Jilin), another splendid reserve covering 1,900km² with original boreal forest, and again on the border of Jilin Province and North Korea. It protects relatively unaltered mixed forests, as well as northeast China's highest mountain (Baiyun, 2,691m) and a splendid crater lake over 370m deep. The mammals here include leopard, lynx, brown and Asiatic black bears, sika and red deer, Chinese goral, wild pig, otter and sable. Notable special birds are black and hazel grouse, black stork, mandarin duck, Oriental stork and scaly-sided merganser.

Dalian Banhaibao NR (Liaoning) is a coastal reserve at the southern tip of the province, some 20km from Dalian city, created mainly to help safeguard the spotted seal.

Shedao-Laotieshan NR (Liaoning). The hill forests of Laotieshan lie on a peninsula south of Dalian. The reserve includes Shedao (Snake Island). Protected species include Pallas's pit viper (*Gloydius halys*), Chinese egret (*Egretta eulophotes*), cranes and mandarin duck.

Top Scaly-sided merganser preening. (MW)
Above Whooper swan flapping wings.

169

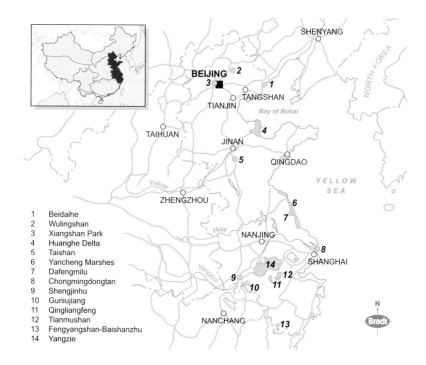

1   Beidaihe
2   Wulingshan
3   Xiangshan Park
4   Huanghe Delta
5   Taishan
6   Yancheng Marshes
7   Dafengmilu
8   Chongmingdongtan
9   Shengjinhu
10 Guniujiang
11 Qingliangfeng
12 Tianmushan
13 Fengyangshan-Baishanzhu
14 Yangzie

4. LOWLAND AND WETLAND REGION OF EAST CHINA (14 SITES)

This coastal region in the east is mainly lowland, with major river basins and numerous lakes and tributaries. In the north, the Yellow River flows into the Bay of Bohai, in the centre the lowlands and lakes are mainly associated with the Huai River, while the south of the region is centred around the tributaries and flood plains of the lower Yangtze River, which reaches the sea just north of Shanghai.

Much of the land has rich alluvial soils and has long been intensively cultivated, and there is also a great deal of industry. It is also highly populated, containing the major cities of Beijing and Shanghai. Nevertheless, there are sites here of great wildlife interest. Notable among them is the coastal site of Beidaihe, famed for its flocks of migrating wildfowl, cranes, waders and other birds. In parts of the west there are some areas of higher ground and forested hills such as Wulingshan, and the relatively isolated highland of central Shandong peaks at Taishan (1,524m). But the main areas of natural history interest here are the wetlands, and these include the important alligator reserve in Anhui.

Here the natural climax vegetation away from wet and flooded soils would be deciduous broadleaf forest with oaks such as *Quercus acutissima* and *Q. variabilis*, elms and limes. However, all but a few remnants have long since been cleared or replaced by secondary woodland, often featuring red pine.

The silt carried to the sea by the Yellow River, and which gives it its name, is steadily deposited at the delta to produce saltmarshes and mudflats, habitats that are highly attractive to migrating waterfowl and waders.

Some of the remaining fragments of natural forest in the south of the region are extremely rich, with the genera *Castanopsis, Liriodendron, Lithocarpus, Litsea, Magnolia, Sophora* and some *Cunninghamia* typical. Ginkgo also still grows in the region, though truly wild examples are very rare.

Beidaihe (Hebei) is a wetland on the coast east of Beijing, best visited in May, or from September through November. It is internationally known amongst keen birders because it is a hot spot for migrants, notably cranes, wildfowl and waders. Many interesting songbirds pass through in the spring, but the finest bird show is in autumn when common, hooded (*Grus monacha*), white-naped, red-crowned and Siberian cranes appear. Other special migrants are Amur falcon (*Falco amurensis*), pied harrier and Oriental stork.

Inland, **Wulingshan NR** (Beijing Shi) is a rare relic of original hill forest not far north of the capital. Mixed deciduous species include oaks, birch, maple, larch and locust tree, and there is even the occasional ginkgo. The mammals include rhesus macaque, musk deer and Chinese goral. Also close to Beijing is **Xiangshan Park** (Beijing Shi), also known as Fragrant Hills. Being so easy of access, it is regularly visited by local tourists. Nevertheless, it is well worth sampling for its beauty and wildlife. In the autumn the colours of the deciduous trees such as maples, poplars and aspens make a splendid display, and it is a very good place to see woodland birds such as red-billed blue magpie and plain laughingthrush (*Garrulax davidi*).

Huanghe Delta NR (Shandong) lies at the mouth of the Yellow River and is notable for its migrating cranes, and for the rare Saunders's gull.

Taishan WHS (Shandong) lies right at the centre of the province. It rises to a peak of 1,545m and is rather a popular scenic spot. Culturally significant and a place of pilgrimage, it is considered a 'birthplace of Chinese civilisation' and is dotted with temples and geological sites. Though the forests here are mostly secondary and degraded, it has warm-temperate hill forests and there are interesting ancient cypresses, pines and pagoda trees. It is also a good spot for woodland birds.

Further south down the coast is **Yancheng Marshes NR MAB** (Jiangsu), China's largest coastal wetland reserve, with marshes, grassland and mudflats, and some temperate woodland. Some 40% of the global population of red-crowned cranes winter here. This is also a breeding site for the threatened Saunders's gull, while black-faced spoonbills (*Platalea minor*) visit in winter. There are plantations of locust tree, dawn redwood and Chinese fir. Unfortunately, the area is threatened by shrimp-and clam-farming.

Nearby **Dafengmilu NR** (Jiangsu) protects saline coastal meadows, its main claim to fame being its captive-bred population of Père David's deer and also Chinese water deer, both rare mammals native to this region. The reed parrotbill is a local special bird found here in the reedbeds.

Another good coastal site is **Chongmingdongtan NR** (Shanghai Shi) with its mudflats, creeks, saltmarshes and reedbeds. The waters are important for fish,

Underside of Chinese sturgeon showing underslung mouth.

including the Chinese sturgeon, and the mudflats and marshes attract large numbers of migrant waders, wildfowl and cranes. The dainty pheasant-tailed jacana may also be spotted here.

Shengjinhu NR (Anhui) is a system of wetlands in the Yangtze River floodplain that attracts large numbers of wildfowl, including wintering cranes, swans and geese.

Guniujiang NR (Anhui) is a forest reserve, with notable birds such as Elliot's pheasant and brown-chested jungle-flycatcher (*Rhinomyias brunneata*). Nearby **Qingliangfeng NR** and **Tianmushan NR MAB** (Zhejiang) also protect subtropical humid hill forests. In the latter, the altitude ranges from 240 to 1,556m, and the rich mixed forests include some ancient (possibly native) gingko trees, and groves of bamboo.

Longwang Shan NR (Dragon King Mountain) (Zhejiang) preserves about 500km^2 of old mountain forest habitats on the slopes of the Tianmushan range, at an altitude of between 450 and 1,580m, some 75km southwest of Shanghai. The vegetation here ranges from subtropical to temperate, with mainly deciduous broadleaf and mixed evergreen broadleaf forest. The variety of trees alone in these forests is amazing, including several species of oak, beech and sweet chestnut, but also magnolias and *Liriodendron*. Animals include leopard, Elliot's pheasant, sika deer, Asiatic black bear, rhesus macaque, hwamei and red-billed blue magpie.

Fengyangshan-Baishanzhu NR (Zhejiang) in the far south of the province is another fine reserve with rich subtropical hill forests, the haunt of Cabot's tragopan and Elliot's pheasant.

Yangze (Chinese Alligator) NR (Anhui) was established in 1982 specifically to protect this rare reptile. Three rivers flow through the reserve, all draining into the Yangtze, with many ditches and ponds providing ideal alligator habitat. There is also a captive breeding and release programme centred here, and efforts are being made to reintroduce this charismatic animal.

Chinese alligator captive breeding programmes are now underway at the Yangtze Chinese Alligator Reserve, to help safeguard the future of this unique and iconic reptile.

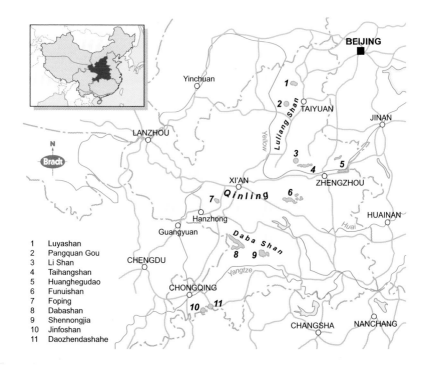

1   Luyashan
2   Pangquan Gou
3   Li Shan
4   Taihangshan
5   Huanghegudao
6   Funuishan
7   Foping
8   Dabashan
9   Shennongjia
10 Jinfoshan
11 Daozhendashahe

5. MOUNTAIN AND FOREST REGION OF CENTRAL CHINA (11 SITES)

This region, at the heart of China, features mainly hills, plains and low mountain ranges. The area has had a high human population density for hundreds of years and was the economic, cultural and political centre of Chinese civilisation. In the north the natural vegetation is for the most part deciduous broadleaf forest dominated by oak. However, there is little primary vegetation remaining, and most of the trees and forests are secondary or planted by man. Here the fauna is typical of temperate woodland, with deer, foxes, badgers and pheasants characteristic.

The dominant forests of this region are temperate deciduous broadleaf, with oak (*Quercus*), lime (*Tilia*), maple (*Acer*) and birch (*Betula*), and ash (*Fraxinus*) and elms (*Ulmus* and *Celtis*) at lower altitudes. At higher levels the dominants would typically be spruce, rowan (*Sorbus*), aspen (*Populus tremula*) and willows (*Salix* spp.). Degraded scrub communities are commoner than forest, and feature hazel (*Corylus* spp.), *Vitex negundo*, *Ostryopsis davidiana* and *Spiraea pubescens*.

The reserves, which protect the remaining remnants of the original forest are highly valued in this heavily urbanised region. Often such reserves are on mountain ranges such as the Luliang Mountains of central Shanxi. Here the forests have a good mixture of conifers such as spruce and also the local Prince Rupprecht's larch (*Larix principis-rupprechtii*). Special birds here include brown eared-pheasant, black stork and mandarin duck.

The region is drained by the Yellow and Yangtze rivers whose broad valleys once supported natural mixed forests on the drier sites. Sadly, few remnants remain. Shaanxi Province, for example, on the loess soils in the north of this region was historically well wooded, but forest now covers a mere 5% of its land.

In the south of the region in Chongqing, the Yangtze valley is also highly populated. Here the climate is humid and subtropical. The original vegetation was evergreen broadleaf forest, except on higher hills where conifers predominated. The rainfall is generally higher than 750mm, rice is the main crop and plantations and farmland dominate in the lowlands. The fauna is of subtropical composition with species such as leopard, sambar, black muntjac, monkeys and pheasants. There are also several endemic species, such as Chinese water deer, giant salamander and Cabot's tragopan. Population pressure, pollution, over-hunting and trapping are major threats to the wildlife in the region.

In the southwest of this region, the main mountains are the Daba and Qinling ranges, forming a watershed between the two great river systems. South of these mountains the forests are mostly subtropical and evergreen in nature, while to the north they are very much temperate and deciduous.

The Qinling Mountains stretch from southern Shaanxi into southwest Henan and reach 3,700m. This is an area with cold winters, and the fauna and flora are distinctly temperate with deciduous forest on the lower slopes which contain oak,

Red or lesser panda eating bamboo, Wolong, Sichuan Province.

elm, walnut, ash and maple trees. Higher up, conifers tend to dominate, pine and birch communities giving way still higher to fir and larch, with shrubs such as rhododendrons. The area is the easternmost limit of giant pandas, and other interesting mammals are takin, golden snub-nosed monkey, red panda and clouded leopard. Dabashan forests feature a mix of evergreen and deciduous trees, with Chinese red pine at higher altitudes.

Luyashan NR in north Shanxi protects remnants of the original mixed forests of the region. This is a site for the very rare brown eared-pheasant.

The Luliang Mountains of central Shanxi Province contain the **Pangquan Gou NR**, another breeding ground for the brown eared-pheasant.

Lying close to the Huang He (Yellow River) in southern Shanxi Province is **Li Shan NR**. Li Shan supports warm-temperate forest that is the habitat for several rare vertebrates including rhesus macaque, musk deer, giant salamander and Koklass pheasant.

Taihangshan NR in the north of Henan Province has hill forests and is good macaque habitat. To the east is **Huanghegudao NR** (Henan) with its Yellow River wetlands, at the transition zone between warm-temperate and subtropical regions.

On the higher ground to the west, **Funiushan** (Henan) protects 560km² of upland temperate and subtropical evergreen broadleaved forests, at altitudes from 480–2,300m.

Further west still, and we enter giant panda country. **Foping NR MAB** (Shaanxi) has one of the main populations of giant pandas and a fascinating mixture of northern and southern species. Other rare mammals here include takin, golden snub-nosed monkey and leopard, while Reeves's pheasant also occurs. The climate is transitional from subtropical to temperate, allowing rich forest cover and a high diversity of bamboo species.

Further south, **Dabashan NR** (Chongqing Shi) has fine humid subtropical forests, and some impressive limestone pinnacles. Dawn redwood can still be found here, mainly on certain

The Asiatic black bear has a distinctive chest marking.

Jinfoshan NR forests contain some rare trees.

southern slopes, as can dove tree and the rare and local conifer *Taiwania flousiana*.

Southeast of Dabashan is **Shennongjia NR MAB** (Hubei). This reserve, covering a range from 420 to 3,100m, holds intact mixed forests, especially at higher levels, although the lower slopes have been somewhat degraded, so the best forests are mainly found on the steeper slopes. These remaining forests are amazingly rich, and many of the stands are of primary old-growth forests, relatively unaffected by people – a rarity indeed in this part of China. The dense forests hold more than 2,600 species of plant. Some of the more interesting species include dove tree, the rare *Tetracentron sinense, Cercidiphyllum japonicum, Emmenopterys henryi* and *Eucommia ulmoides*. A number of rare mammals are protected here too, including golden snub-nosed monkey (at its eastern limit), leopard, musk deer, wild boar, Asiatic black bear and macaques. Notable birds include Reeves's pheasant.

Legend has it that a humanoid creature (the 'Wild Man of Shennongjia') also inhabits these forested peaks, but its existence has yet to be established, despite numerous alleged sightings. Perhaps the strange golden snub-nosed monkey is at least in part responsible for such stories?

Jinfoshan NR (Chongqing Shi), in the south of the province, also has good mixed forests with many rare plants including dove tree, while **Daozhendashahe NR** (Chongqing Shi) is best known for its karst forests. François' leaf monkey is the most important rare mammal protected here, and others include tufted deer and Chinese muntjac.

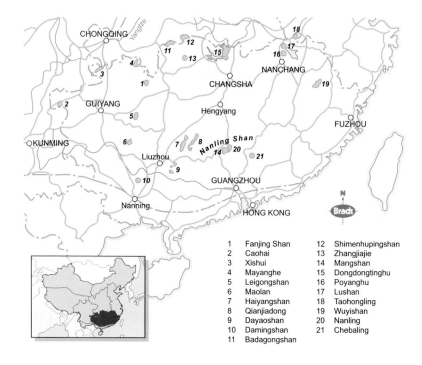

1	Fanjing Shan	12	Shimenhupingshan
2	Caohai	13	Zhangjiajie
3	Xishui	14	Mangshan
4	Mayanghe	15	Dongdongtinghu
5	Leigongshan	16	Poyanghu
6	Maolan	17	Lushan
7	Haiyangshan	18	Taohongling
8	Qianjiadong	19	Wuyishan
9	Dayaoshan	20	Nanling
10	Damingshan	21	Chebaling
11	Badagongshan		

6. MOUNTAIN AND FOREST REGION OF SOUTH CHINA (21 SITES)

This region encompasses the hills and mountain ranges of southeast China, south of the basin of the Yangtze River. The natural vegetation here consists of rich subtropical forests, grading into the broader tropical plains in the south. Forest composition varies with altitude, aspect and geology, and is richly varied, with evergreen broadleaved and coniferous communities as well as deciduous woodland. Groves of bamboo also dominate in patches, and at high levels there are cloud-forests of pine, birch and cypress. Rare birds occuring here include David's parrotbill (*Paradoxornis davidianus*), Elliot's pheasant and the more widespread silver pheasant. While mountains dominate in the southern third, to the north the hills gradually give way to lowland.

Notable mammals here are black-fronted (*Muntiacus crinifrons*) and Reeves's muntjacs, and Chinese water deer in the lowlands of the Yangtze Basin.

Nanling Shan is an important range in the south of this region. The forests here are dominated by oaks, chestnuts and laurels, with cinnamon, elm and many shrubs on the lower slopes. Protected plants here include *Liriodendron chinense*, *Camellia chrysantha* and tree ferns.

Guizhou and neighbouring parts of northern Guangxi to the south and western Hunan to the east are on an undulating plateau at about 1,000–1,400m, featuring steep and often wooded conical limestone peaks – classic and famous Chinese scenery so often featuring in traditional paintings. These were formed when calcareous sedimentary deposits were forced upwards in the Tertiary Period by tectonic activity. This is typical karst country, with caves, sinkholes and rivers that disappear underground in places. Many of the once forested hills have been long denuded, but important remnants can still be found in the reserves. **Fanjing Shan NR** for example protects forest in the northeast of the plateau, and the endemic Guizhou snub-nosed monkey is restricted to this site, where it numbers about 500 individuals.

Other rare mammals of the region include sika deer and just possibly the vanishingly rare south China tiger, as well as macaques, François' leaf monkey, Chinese goral and both leopard and clouded leopard, though these are very rare. Giant salamanders also occur here in the mountain streams. The plants include Chinese fir and rare trees such as dove tree, as well as tree ferns. The geology is largely karst limestone, resulting in some steep slopes and picturesque scattered pinnacles. The original forests were mainly evergreen broadleaf, and featured oaks and relatives (*Castanopsis*, *Cyclobalanopsis* and *Quercus*), with laurels (*Eugenia*, *Phoebe*) and other shrubs such as *Schima* and *Camellia* (tea genus), with figs (*Ficus*), dogwoods (*Cornus*), *Rhus*, *Albizzia* and *Liquidambar*. Further north conifers such as Chinese red pine (*Pinus massoniana*) feature, with Chinese fir, spruce (*Picea*) and fir (*Abies*). The rare endangered conifers *Cathaya argyrophylla* and *Taiwania flousiana* also occur in this region, as does the beautiful dove tree.

The wetlands of northern Jiangxi and northern Hunan are important for wildlife, although this area has been heavily cultivated for centuries, mainly for rice. Mammals of these wetlands include otter and Chinese water deer. These rivers and lakes are also noted as the last refuge of the probably extinct Yangtze river dolphin, Chinese and white sturgeons and giant salamander. However, in addition to agricultural run-off and severe pollution, the whole lower Yangtze River Basin is being affected by the enormous Three Gorges Dam project. The ecological repercussions of its construction are as yet unknown, though unlikely to be beneficial to wildlife.

Caohai NR (Guizhou) is a famous high-altitude lake in the west of the province, best known for its waterfowl and other visiting birds, most notably bar-headed goose, ruddy shelduck, black-necked crane and eastern imperial eagle.

Xishui NNR (Guizhou) lies on the border with Sichuan and protects good subtropical evergreen broadleaved forest. Further east, **Mayanghe NR** (Guizhou) is famous mainly as the site for François' leaf monkey, the colony consisting of about 500 individuals.

In the southeast of the province is **Leigongshan NR** (Guizhou), protecting another, slightly larger area of subtropical hill forest. The smaller reserve of **Maolan NR MAB** (Guizhou), on the southern border with Guangxi, features subtropical forest in a karst landscape with many streams and lakes, the haunt of musk deer and rhesus macaques. The rare fairy pitta and silver oriole are found here. Maolan is the best karst forest in China and is also famous for the diversity of orchid species.

Due east of the famous tourist destination of Guilin lies **Haiyangshan NR** (Guangxi), an area of hills and forests preserved partly for water catchment. A little further east is the border hill forest reserve of **Qianjiadong NR** (Guangxi). These forests feature such trees as Chinese yew and *Lithocarpus*. Silver and golden pheasants and Temminck's tragopan have been recorded from the latter.

Dayaoshan NR (Guangxi) is a large reserve of 2,022km^2 and a range from about 100 to about 1,900m. Although it has suffered from logging and hunting, it is still a fine place for wildlife. The mammals here include musk deer, muntjac, serow, rhesus macaque and clouded leopard. The birdlife is very rich too, with Cabot's tragopan, pittas and babblers among many others, and specialities such as gold-fronted fulvetta (*Alcippe chrysotis*) and rosy minivet.

Further to the west is **Damingshan NR** (Guangxi), which has mixed habitats, including rocky areas, deep gorges, remnants of original forest, plateau, scrub and grassland. Notable species here are macaques, squirrels (including a flying squirrel), silver oriole, red-tailed laughingthrush (*Garrulax milnei*), green-billed malkoha, small niltava (*Niltava macgrigoriae*) and Mrs Gould's sunbird. It is most famous among birders because the rare white-eared night heron has been seen here.

Badagongshan NR (Hunan) in the north of the province is a pretty reserve with excellent temperate hill forest, home to leopard, serow, Asiatic black bear and pangolin. Giant salamanders are also found here. Some areas of forest have ancient dove trees. Common birds of the scrub are Elliot's laughingthrush (*Garrulax elliotii*) and white-collared yuhina (*Yuhina diademata*). Koklass, Reeves's and golden pheasants all breed here, as does Temminck's tragopan.

Shimenhupingshan NR (Hupingshan) (Hunan), to the northeast of Badagongshan, has some fine hill forest, with dove trees, and rises to nearly 2,100m, the highest peak in northern Hunan, and the second highest of the province. South China tiger has been seen here, and there are Asiatic black bears and rhesus macaques. The birds include Cabot's tragopan, silver and Koklass pheasants and silver oriole.

Zhangjiajie FP (Hunan) lies a little to the south. This is a well-known tourist spot with picturesque limestone rock formations, but it is also well worth visiting for its wildlife (though avoid peak tourist seasons and public holidays). The mixed forest includes dawn redwood, Chinese yew, dove tree, tree of heaven and *Liquidambar*. Birds include Reeves's pheasant, sulphur-breasted warbler (*Phylloscopus ricketti*), grey-headed canary flycatcher and green-backed tit.

Mangshan NR (Hunan), in the far south, on the Guangdong border, has mixed hill forest, some rather degraded, rocks, crags and a reservoir. Notable birds include parrotbills, varied tit (*Sittiparus varius*), silver oriole and Cabot's tragopan, with spotted forktail (*Enicurus maculatus*) on the rivers.

Dongdongtinghu NR (East Dongting Lake) (Hunan) is one of China's most famous sites. A large freshwater lake, it has been partly drained for farmland. An important refuge for wildlife, especially in winter, it experiences seasonal fluctuations, increasing from about 3,500 to more than 13,000km^2 and by more than 10m depth in summer. The main claim to fame are the flocks of wintering cranes (common, hooded, white-naped and Siberian), storks (Oriental, white and black), and wildfowl including geese and scaly-sided merganser. About 70% of the world population of lesser white-fronted geese winter here.

Above left The male silver pheasant has a showy tail.
Above right The red-tailed laughingthrush lives in evergreen forest. (GG)

Poyanghu NR (Jiangxi). Like Dongdongtinghu, this large lake changes in depth and area between wet summer and dry winter seasons, and as it dries out in the autumn, pools and wet meadows appear, attracting huge numbers of migrant birds. In wet summers it expands to about 5,500km². Up to 4,000 Siberian cranes (95% of the world's population) winter here, as do white-naped and hooded cranes, Oriental stork and swan goose, along with many other geese and ducks, including Baikal teal.

Lushan NR (Jiangxi), just to the north of Poyang, is a well-known mountain with a patchwork of hill forest, some of it well preserved. The wildlife includes pangolin, mandarin duck, yellow-bellied tit, red-billed blue magpie and black bulbul. Nearby **Taohongling NR** (Jiangxi) has a small reservoir and scrubby woodland with bamboo. Best known for its sika deer, the birds include black bitterns (*Ixobrychus flavicollis*) in the paddyfields, and the scrub has striated prinia (*Prinia criniger*) and red-billed starling.

Wuyishan NR WHS MAB (Jiangxi/Fujian) is a beautiful reserve and one of the best wildlife sites in this region. It is large (565km²), and has a splendidly wide range of forest types. Subtropical broadleaf forest with *Lithocarpus* dominates to about 1,200m, with bamboo patches in the undergrowth; above this to about 1,700m it is mostly coniferous with Chinese cedar, Chinese yew, Chinese fir and pines (*Pinus massoniana*); higher still this thins out to thickets of willow and juniper and eventually to alpine grassland. The rivers and streams have brown dippers and white-capped water redstarts. Local special birds are chestnut-vented nuthatch (*Sitta nagaensis*), rosy pipit (*Anthus roseatus*), spotted wren-babbler (*Spelaeornis formosus*) and green shrike-babbler (*Pteruthius xanthochlorus*).

Nanling NR (Guangdong) protects mainly subtropical evergreen hill forest, as does nearby **Chebaling NR** (Guangdong). The latter has arguably the best lowland forest in the province, and is justly popular with birders and other naturalists. This is a splendid reserve in which the rare south China tiger may still roam, along with clouded leopard and Asiatic golden cat. Special birds here are white-eared night heron, Blyth's and crested kingfishers and silver pheasant.

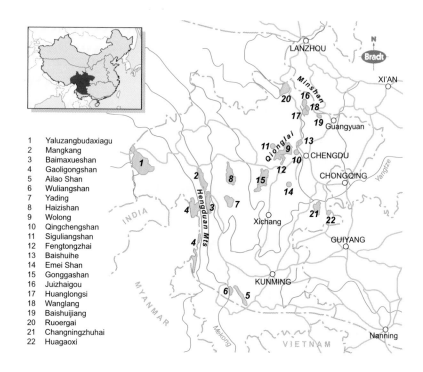

1 Yaluzangbudaxiagu
2 Mangkang
3 Baimaxueshan
4 Gaoligongshan
5 Ailao Shan
6 Wuliangshan
7 Yading
8 Haizishan
9 Wolong
10 Qingchengshan
11 Siguliangshan
12 Fengtongzhai
13 Baishuihe
14 Emei Shan
15 Gonggashan
16 Juizhaigou
17 Huanglongsi
18 Wanglang
19 Baishuijiang
20 Ruoergai
21 Changningzhuhai
22 Huagaoxi

7. MOUNTAINS OF SOUTHWEST CHINA (22 SITES)

This region is dominated by high ground in the west and south, and by the large Sichuan Basin in the northeast. The eastern extension of the Tibetan Plateau dominates in southeast Tibet and adjacent west Sichuan, and high ground is also a feature of northern Yunnan. At lower altitudes here the main vegetation consists of tropical and subtropical moist broadleaf forests, developed under the influence of the rainy southeast monsoons. The higher altitude results in generally cooler, moister conditions, with coniferous forests persisting in patches. It is a geographically complex area of sub tropical to sub alpine mountains divided by major river gorges. The mountains of southwest China contain about 12,000 species of plant, of which 3,500 are endemic (ie: found nowhere else). This is the richest biodiversity of all temperate regions.

The Minshan and Qionglai mountain ranges are at the eastern edge of the Tibetan Plateau, and include steep valleys and also some high peaks at above 7,500m, the highest peak being glacier-clad Gongga Shan at 7,556m. The relatively cool and misty conditions at moderate altitudes here support superb mixed forest with patches of bamboo – ideal habitat for that most charismatic of all China's mammals, the giant panda. Here a series of reserves protects the panda and its rich forest home so successfully that numbers of this marvellous animal seem at last to be on the rise. Above the trees there are areas dominated by many species of rhododendron, with roses and *Berberis*, and alpine habitats dominate from about 4,000m.

The Hengduan and adjacent mountains have altitudes ranging from below 1,000m in the valley floors to glacial peaks of above 6,000m on the highest ridges. Thus the area has spectacular scenery with raging rivers, gorges and a very rich flora and fauna. The vegetation ranges from subtropical evergreen broadleaf forest at lower altitudes through deciduous temperate broadleaf forests, mixed broadleaf conifer forests, coniferous sub-alpine forests with dense bamboo and rhododendron, to alpine meadows above the tree line. The dominant conifers in the mountain forests between 2,800 and 4,000m are hemlock, spruce, fir and larch, and rhododendrons feature in the shrub-layer. In general, fir tends to take over from spruce above about 3,500m. Bamboos, ferns, mosses and lichens are abundant in the moister, humid sites and the curious lichen *Usnea longissima* hangs down from tree branches in some places, looking like 'Spanish moss'.

These mountains, in northern Yunnan, the extreme southeast of Tibet and western Sichuan, contain about half of all China's plant species and are rich in endemics. The Hengduan Mountains alone, covering about 500,000km^2, contain around 9,000 plant species with a high proportion of endemics, and have been designated a biodiversity hotspot. The isolation of individual ridges of high ground from others nearby by deep river valleys is thought to have been partly responsible for the high levels of speciation in the area. Big changes in climate over short distances are a feature here. Thus there are patches of subtropical monsoon forest on certain lower-altitude slopes, between about 1,000 and 1,500m, and alpine habitats topped by permanent snow at 5,000m and above. These mountains host between 30–40% of the world's species of several plant genera, such as *Gentiana*, *Primula* and *Rhododendron*.

The fauna is extremely rich too, and is composed of Palaearctic species at higher altitudes and Indo-Malayan species at lower altitudes. There are large numbers of special endemic species, including giant panda, golden snub-nosed monkey and many species of pheasant. Other mammals found here include takin, stump-tailed macaque, tufted deer, Indian muntjac, jungle cat (*Felis chaus*), spotted linsang, clouded leopard, Asiatic black bear and red panda. Special plants here include dawn redwood, Chinese yew, *Manglietia fordiana* and Chinese cedar (*Cryptomeria fortunei*).

Locally restricted and endemic birds are a major feature of this region. Laughingthrushes are particularly well represented here, with barred (*Garrulax lunulatus*), Elliot's, giant (*G. maximus*) and white-speckled (*G. bieti*) being specialities of the area, as are Chinese (*Turdus mupinensis*) and Kessler's thrushes (*T. kessleri*), Sichuan partridge (*Arborophila rufipectus*), Sichuan jay, three-banded rosefinch (*Carpodacus trifasciatus*) and Yunnan nuthatch. This is also the centre of pheasant diversity.

The picturesque ancient town of Lijiang, in the northwest of Yunnan, lies not far from the magnificent snow-topped range of Yulong Xue Shan (Jade Dragon Snow Mountain), rising to a height of 5,596m and still unconquered! A visit to the mountain includes an ascent by ski-lift to Yunshan Meadow for a closer view of this impressive massif, with its permanent glacier, the most southerly in China. This is a famous botanical site, with a rich flora. The lower slopes have interesting vegetation, including *Berberis* and *Cotoneaster*, and at higher altitudes the flowers include paeonies and clematis. In the woods around the top of the ski-lift station there are species of *Clematis*, *Corydalis*, *Iris* and *Primula*.

The western parts of the plateau, where forested, tend to support secondary stands of Yunnan pine, often with rhododendrons in the undergrowth. The latter are a delight for visiting botanists (and gardeners) in spring and summer.

The Sichuan Basin in east Sichuan and neighbouring Chongching is heavily populated, with well over 100 million inhabitants. Indeed human settlement here goes back more than 5,000 years and the low, fertile land is also heavily agricultural. Nevertheless, Yunnan as a whole is one of the richest of China's provinces in terms of biodiversity. Bordered in the west by Myanmar and to the south by Laos and Vietnam, it has a remarkable range in altitude from about 75m in the southeast to over 5,400m near the border with Tibet in the northwest. Much of it is a huge upland plateau, connecting to the Tibetan foothills via the Hengduan Mountains in the north. The altitude falls gradually towards the south, the habitats becoming increasingly tropical. The plateau itself has a mild climate, the subtropical latitude being ameliorated by the altitude, which varies between about 1,700 and 2,300m. The natural vegetation is mainly evergreen broadleaved forest, but most has been removed or replaced with forestry. Logging and over-grazing linked with population pressure have been the major threats to biodiversity. Some of the higher ridges support fern- and moss-rich cloudforest with bamboo.

The tufted deer has white-tipped ears.

The **Three Parallel Rivers Protected Area** is probably Yunnan's most important wildlife refuge. Three great rivers – Salween (Nujiang), Mekong (Lancang Jiang) and Yangtze (Jinsha Jiang) – flow close together and almost parallel, in a mountainous landscape where the habitats range from alpine to sub tropical. The protected areas include Gaoligong Mountain (514,022ha), Baima-Meili Snow Mountain (349,019ha), Laowo Mountain (49,161ha), Laojun Mountain (131,427ha), Yunling Mountain (89,787ha), Red Mountain (364,687 ha) and Haba Mountain (200,315ha).

Here are some of south China's finest and richest forests, and this is also the place of origin of many familiar garden flowers, including gentians, lilies and orchids. Rare mammals include Tibetan watershrew, the endemic Yunnan snub-nosed monkey, capped leaf monkey, wild dog, red panda, Asiatic black bear, smooth-coated otter, leopard, clouded leopard and even the elusive snow leopard on the high slopes. Other notable mammals include musk deer, takin and red and Chinese gorals.

The birds are equally fascinating, with Lady Amherst's and blood pheasants, white eared-pheasant, Sclater's monal, Blyth's tragopan, black-necked crane, Ward's trogon, giant and Yunnan nuthatches, white-speckled laughingthrush and brown-winged parrotbill (*Paradoxornis brunneus*).

Yaluzangbudaxiagu NR (Yaluzangbu Great Canyon) (Tibet) lies in the southeast of Tibet, and is an alpine valley with tropical influences. This huge canyon holds splendid forests, rich in species.

Mangkang NR (Tibet), on the border with the far north of Yunnan, protects the mountain spruce and fir forests that are the habitat of the rare Yunnan snub-nosed monkey, one of China's most treasured endemic mammals. These wonderful primates are also protected in **Baimaxueshan NR** (Yunnan), a little to the south, which also has fine temperate and cold-temperate mountain forests and scrub.

Despite their dazzling plumage, golden pheasants can be hard to see.

Gaoligongshan NR MAB (Yunnan). This splendid reserve is of great international ecological importance for its range of habitats and rich biodiversity. Covering the crest of a narrow mountain range in northwest Yunnan, it features largely unaltered forest strata, from subtropical, humid evergreen broadleaf forest to subalpine conifer forest. Warm temperate evergreen broadleaf forests of oak and laurel at 2,000m are replaced by cold temperate deciduous forests and conifer forests above 3,000m. *Taiwania flousiana* is a rare conifer that is locally dominant at 2,200m to 2,400m in some forests here in humid sites. Associated trees include *Tsuga dumosa*, *Pinus griffithii*, *Cyclobalanopsis glauca* and *Magnolia* spp. The mammals include red panda and clouded leopard, and notable birds are Sclater's monal, Hume's pheasant (*Syrmaticus humiae*) and green peafowl.

In the mountains of subtropical central Yunnan lie two major reserves. **Ailao Shan NR** (Yunnan) has a population of black gibbons, a severely threatened species, as well as Asiatic black bears. Today Yunnan pine covers many of the slopes – often planted, but possibly native in some sites. Many local birds inhabit this region, notably Yunnan and giant nuthatch, white-speckled laughingthrush, Hume's pheasant, white eared-pheasant, brown-winged parrotbill and green peafowl.

Silhouetted conifers at dawn from Elephant Washing Pool on Emei Shan.

Nearby **Wuliangshan NR** (Yunnan) with its evergreen broadleaf forest is also very rich. It is another good spot for pheasants and also for the rather local giant nuthatch.

Sichuan Province, comparable with Yunnan in its wildlife richness, has a string of splendid sites. Near the Yunnan border is **Yading NR MAB** (Sichuan) with its complex array of habitats, and altitudes range from 2,200 to 6,032m. Here there are fine subalpine and alpine forests, alpine bush and grassland, home to leopard, black bear, Asiatic golden cat and golden pheasant. This reserve includes a number of Buddhist temples and the area is sacred to the locals who live mainly in harmony with the wildlife. To the north, **Haizishan NR** (Sichuan) protects a larger area with mountain forests, glacier and alpine lakes. This is famed as a site for the endemic white-lipped deer.

A group of reserves in the **Qionglai Mountains** of central Sichuan are world famous, and justly so. This is classic giant panda country, and includes the flagship reserve of **Wolong NR MAB** with its panda breeding centre. This reserve, not far from Chengdu in Sichuan Province, is the most famous of China's giant panda reserves. The reserve is home to about 100 wild pandas. The climate is one of long snowy winters (November to March) and rather cool, wet summers. Largest (2,000km²) and best known of the giant panda reserves, Wolong preserves a vast array of forests, from mixed subtropical broadleaf forests on the lower slopes at about 1,000m, through temperate forests at higher levels, and subalpine conifer stands higher still, with open alpine communities above the treeline at 3,000m and more. The highest peak (6,250m) has permanent ice. The famous giant pandas roam through these bamboo-rich forests but are unlikely to be spotted as they are thinly spread and solitary. The panda breeding centre offers good views though, and there is an interesting museum. The birds are interesting here too, specialities including black-throated blue robin (*Luscinia obscura*) and Chinese monal. The vegetation includes familiar garden plants such as *Cotoneaster horizontalis* and *Buddleia davidii*, both wild here. Familiar trees such as oaks, birch and beech are mixed with less familiar species such as walnut, wingnut (*Pterocarya*) and *Sophora*. Higher up there are hemlock (*Tsuga*), spruce (*Picea*) and larch (*Larix*), with lime (*Tilia chinensis*) and cherry, and higher still fir (*Abies*), with birch and rhododendrons, grading to juniper and alpine meadows.

Closer still to Chengdu is **Qingchengshan WHS** (Sichuan), a beautiful reserve of wooded mountains, protecting one of China's best-preserved subtropical evergreen forests, with fine stands of the rare dove tree. Revered as the birthplace of Taoism, it is probably the religious significance that has given it protection down the centuries. The mountain contains several well-preserved temples, scattered around the lakes and forests. The mixed vegetation and abundance of flowering shrubs make it a fine spot to see butterflies and woodland birds. **Siguliangshan** (Sichuan) to the west of Wolong has fine alpine forests, glacier and lakes. Also close is **Fengtongzhai NR** (Sichuan) with its subtropical hill forests, and just to the north the small **Baishuihe NR**.

Something of an outlier to the southeast is the famed **Emei Shan WHS** (Sichuan). Rising to 3,100m this mountain is a sacred Buddhist site – a fact which has helped to preserve its habitats. There are dozens of monasteries that can be reached along a winding track. It is one of the best places to see the remnants of the

Travertine terraces are part of the karst landscape at Huanglong WHS MAB.

original subtropical forests and it is blessed with a number of special animals and plants, either endemic or found in only a few other sites. Local special plants include dove tree, the evergreen *Nothophoebe omeiensis* and *Rosa omeiensis*. The stump-tailed macaque is also found here. It has longer hair than the much commoner rhesus macaque. The local birds are particularly special and include the rare Emei Shan liocichla (*Liocichla omeiensis*), parrotbills and white-browed (*Poecile superciliosa*), rusty-bellied (*P. davidi*) and sooty tits (*Aegithalos fuliginosus*). **Gonggashan** (Sichuan) to the south has stunning scenery, with areas of well-preserved coniferous forests, and alpine habitats above the tree line. This glacier-clad peak is Sichuan's highest – a truly impressive 7,556m.

Further north lies the **Minshan range**. The most famous sites here are very popular with internal tourists, so public holidays are best avoided, but they are stunning and full of wildlife. These are **Jiuzhaigou WHS/NR MAB** and **Huanglongsi WHS/NR MAB**. The landscape here is remarkable, set amidst montane forest, and ringed by mountains. The centrepiece is a series of clear unpolluted cascading pools, waterfalls and streams, on calcite terraces, with a backdrop of forests, hills and mountain peaks. The pools shimmer in different shades of orange, yellow, green and blue, caused by a range of algae and bacteria.

The forests (some of which contain giant pandas) are mainly of Chinese hemlock (*Tsuga chinensis*), various species of spruce, including Chinese spruce (*Picea asperata*), firs (*Abies*), birches (*Betula*) and larches (*Larix*). The general flora is rich and noted for the many species of slipper orchid, such as *Cypripedium flavum*, *tibeticum* and *bardolphianum*. Notable birds are Chinese monal and Sichuan jay. Huanglongsi is a holy site for Tibetan Buddhists and Taoists and has a fine temple. Both of these reserves are tourist honeypots, but the area is large and it is possible to escape the hordes of visitors and enjoy one of China's finest natural areas. **Wanglang NR** was established to protect giant pandas, of which about 60 survive here or in the adjacent forest outside the reserve. Other mammals here are golden snub-nosed monkey, takin, leopard, fox, lynx, red panda, musk deer, blue sheep and pikas. Visitors can walk through rhododendron and pine forests, and a species list of plants is available at Wanglang Forest Lodge. To the east, on the border with Gansu, is **Baishuijiang NR MAB**. For its size, this reserve has one of the largest populations of giant pandas, numbering possibly about 100. Birds include the very local snowy-cheeked laughingthrush (*Garrulax sukatschewi*). The rich mixed forests here feature cinnamon, oak, poplar, birch, spruce and fir, with rich growths of bamboo and rhododendron.

To the northwest of Jiuzhaigou lies **Ruoergai NR** (Sichuan), a large reserve featuring high-altitude marshes and other peat-rich wetlands. In fact this is the world's largest highland peat area and is a habitat for endangered species such as black-necked crane and Pallas's gull, as well as pikas and Himalayan marmots.

In the far south of Sichuan, near the border with Guizhou, two reserves display the range of habitats found in this amazingly varied province. **Changningzhuhai NR** (Changning Bamboo 'Sea') has the largest natural bamboo forest in China covering over 100km², notably the tall mosu bamboo. The relatively small reserve of **Huagaoxi NR** protects mixed hill forests in this humid subtropical region.

Giant panda feeding on bamboo in mountain habitat in Wolong.

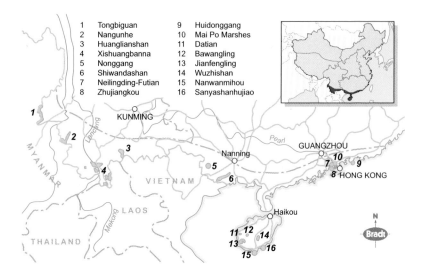

1	Tongbiguan	9	Huidonggang
2	Nangunhe	10	Mai Po Marshes
3	Huanglianshan	11	Datian
4	Xishuangbanna	12	Bawangling
5	Nonggang	13	Jianfengling
6	Shiwandashan	14	Wuzhishan
7	Neilingding-Futian	15	Nanwanmihou
8	Zhujiangkou	16	Sanyashanhujiao

8. TROPICAL REGION OF SOUTH CHINA (16 SITES)

The tropical zone of China is rather small, consisting of the south and west of Yunnan, a narrow band along the southern coasts of Guangxi and Guangdong as well as Macao, Hong Kong and the island of Hainan. Soils in the zone are mostly acidic and the climate is typically humid throughout the year. The natural vegetation of the region is tropical evergreen forest, dominated by dipterocarp tree species in the sheltered valleys, semi-evergreen forests on other low-lying areas, and subtropical evergreen broadleaf forests on the hills. The rainfall is rather high, ranging between 1,200mm and 3,000mm a year. Deciduous monsoon forests occur in some western areas, while montane evergreen forests and cloudforests occur on the highest peaks.

The forests in the more sheltered parts of southwest Hainan and Yunnan are very tall and luxuriant. Mammals found here include the occasional Asian elephant, gaur, binturong, slow loris, leaf monkeys and gibbons, and tropical birds include hornbills, peacocks, broadbills and pittas. Biologically these are the richest and most diverse habitats in China, but also unfortunately some of the most fragile. Much of the natural vegetation has been destroyed, the major threats to biodiversity being deforestation and the unsustainable use of resources.

In southern Yunnan, in Xishuangbanna, the landscape becomes gradually greener and lower, the hills clad with forest or given over to plantations of rubber, tea and tropical fruits, while in the valleys and basins rice paddies shimmer in the sunshine. Lying sandwiched between Myanmar and Laos, well to the south of the Tropic of Cancer, it is a fertile landscape dominated by tropical forests, and drained by the mighty Lancang (upper Mekong) River and its tributaries. The altitude ranges from 420m to 2,400m and the rainfall is still generally high, between 1,200 and 1,700mm per year, falling mainly from May to October. Xishuangbanna is the only area in China with a large amount of relatively undisturbed tropical forest, and consequently it has a high biodiversity. Forests are important to the local people, and more than 65% of the land is still covered by forest or scrub of one sort or another. Most of this is either secondary growth or significantly altered from its original state, often replaced by bamboo, rubber plantation or grassland. The rivers here are fast-flowing, and frequently the water is opaque and red-brown due to the effects of soil erosion.

Soil erosion has become worse with the replacement of forest and removal of natural ground cover. At somewhat higher altitudes, between about 800m and 1,000m, the natural cover is a monsoon semi-evergreen forest. Here the emergent trees shed their leaves in the dry season, but the lower layers are mainly evergreen.

Although large tracts of tropical forest do remain, many of the hills here are covered with rubber plantations. Fortunately though, the Chinese government now supports the traditional lifestyles of the Dai people, very much to the benefit of conservation, and earlier efforts to extend the rubber plantations enormously at the expense of the natural or managed forests have thankfully been largely abandoned. That said, China's huge and expanding car industry has led to an increased demand for rubber in recent years. Rubber is still a major crop here, sometimes undercropped with coffee, and there are also plantations of pineapple and lychee.

The rubber trees are also used as firewood, as are *Cassia siamea* trees, which are planted by the villagers in special fuelwood groves and coppiced regularly for a supply of logs and poles. The *Cassia* trees quickly produce fresh growth from the stumps.

The local philosophy reveres nature, certain areas being designated as sacred, and these are traditionally conserved. In some Dai communities individual trees, usually sacred fig and lofty fig, are revered. Almost every village in Xishuangbanna has sacred trees, which are the location for performance of rituals and traditional ceremonies. A distinction can be made between sacred trees dating back to pre-Buddhist, animistic beliefs, and those attributable to Buddhism. The former grow wild, and are worshipped through collective rituals, whereas the latter are planted, and are often worshipped in individual acts. Sacred fig is usually planted as a sacred tree for family cult activities, and can often be found near villages.

Tropical and sub tropical crops grow well in the fertile soil, farmers enjoying two or three harvests a year. Home to the famous Pu'er tea, the region also produces quinine, rubber, camphor, coffee, cocoa and a wide range of food crops, including pineapple, mango, banana, plantain, cashew and coconut.

Its warm, humid forests and nature reserves are home to gaur and even the occasional Asian elephant (there are about 200 elephants in this region). There are also gibbons, peacocks, leopards, lorises and tree shrews. Interesting birds to be seen in the area include Asian palm swift, Himalayan swiftlet (whose nests are still eaten as bird's nest soup in some areas), red-whiskered bulbul, speckled piculet, bronzed drongo, sunbirds, bush robins and hornbills. Conservation is becoming more of a priority nowadays, not least to meet the lucrative eco tourist trade, and over a quarter of a million hectares of forest is now designated as reserve.

Most of Guangxi is subtropical, supporting evergreen forests with trees such as *Castanopsis* and *Cryptocaria*, with *Liquidambar* in some parts (mainly in the southwest).

Tropical rainforest in Wild Elephant Valley, Xishuangbanna NR.

The oriental pied hornbill is a bird of the tropical zone.

In the northern mountains the mixed forests have deciduous broadleaf trees including oaks, whilst in the deep south there are monsoon rainforests with trees such as *Dracontomelon*. The province is much less well known than Yunnan, yet is also extremely rich in wildlife. The coastal mangroves close to the border between Guangxi and Guangdong still support small numbers of dugong.

Much of Hong Kong would naturally carry subtropical evergreen forest, but it suffered heavy deforestation in the past. Thankfully reforestation projects have been put in place since. Grasslands and patches of secondary forest dominate here, although the **Tai Po Kau NR** retains a small patch of possibly semi-original forest.

Other important nature reserves in Hong Kong include Hoi Ha Wan, a marine reserve with coral reefs, the mangrove-rich marshes and restored fishponds of Mai Po, and the islands of Lamma and Lantau. Marine turtles breed on some of the sandy beaches and the rare Chinese dolphin still occurs in the murky waters of the Pearl River estuary. This is a form of the Indo-Pacific hump-backed dolphin, which here is a striking pinkish colour when adult.

The island province of Hainan is the second largest of China's coastal islands, after Taiwan. Its climate is tropical, with a moist, monsoonal summer and a cooler, drier winter. Over its million-year history many endemic species have evolved here. In all there are 4,200 plant species (of which about 630 are endemic), about 100 mammal species and 300 species of bird (of which nearly 50 are endemic). Although much of the original forest has been destroyed, especially around the coasts, the mountainous interior still has considerable tracts of mainly dry-deciduous monsoon forest. The value of nature reserves on Hainan is critical, as the coast has rapidly been developed for tourism and deforestation is a major threat to the interior.

Eld's deer stag and hind at Datian Nature Reserve.

The main trees here, such as *Kleinhovia hospita*, *Spondias pinnata* and the lime *Tilia hainanensis*, drop their leaves to avoid water stress in the dry season. At higher altitudes, above about 1,000m, an evergreen broadleaf forest takes over, with genera such as *Castanopsis*, *Lithocarpus* and *Schima*. The conifers include pines, *Podocarpus* and the threatened *Dacrydium pierrei* and *Cephalotaxus hainanensis*. Notable mammals include black gibbon, the endemic Hainan flying squirrel (*Hylopetes electilis*) and Hainan moonrat (*Neohylomys hainanensis*). Special birds include Hainan leaf warbler and Hainan partridge (*Aborophila ardens*). Other notable birds are crested serpent eagle, bay woodpecker (*Blythipicus pyrrhotis*), chestnut bulbul (*Hemixos castanonotus*), fork-tailed sunbird, pale-capped pigeon (*Columba punicea*) and grey and ratchet-tailed treepies. Although plantations of rubber, eucalyptus, coffee and oilpalm have replaced the natural vegetation in most of Hainan's lowlands, and deforestation affects many of the mountain slopes, there are important remnants of the original forests on some of the mountains such as Bawangling. The latter still supports Hainan gibbon and Hainan partridge. Datian reserve has a population of the rare Eld's deer.

Tongbiguan NR and **Nangunhe NR** are right in the west of Yunnan, close to the border with Myanmar and in the north of the tropical region. The lowland valleys and lower slopes are dominated by tropical rainforest with subtropical evergreen broadleaf forests at higher levels. Further to the southeast is **Huanglianshan NR** (Yunnan) with rich tropical mountain forests. The rare beautiful nuthatch (*Sitta formosa*) has been seen here. Notable species of these border reserves are hoolock gibbon and possibly slow loris and binturong. A survey in early 2004 indicated that there may even be occasional Indochinese tigers in Nanhunge and possibly also in Huangliangshan.

Xishuangbanna NR MAB (Yunnan). This region in Yunnan's far south covers 2,417km² at an altitude range of 420–2,300m. It has a series of five nature reserves

Avocets at Mai Po Marshes NR, Hong Kong .

A green peacock peers out from a forked tree.

(Mengyang, Menglun, Mengla, Shangyong and Mengao) to protect the treasures of the tropical rainforests that still clothe some of the hills and lowlands here. This is the largest of China's tropical forests. Herds of gaur still lurk in the forests and even Asian elephants can sometimes be found, though they are hard to spot and low in numbers. There are also occasional reports of Indochinese tigers. In areas up to about 800m, the natural vegetation is tropical evergreen forest, and in mature stands the largest trees, such as the dipterocarps *Dipterocarpus turbinatus*, *Parashorea sinensis* and *Vatica*, may reach 30 or even 50m. The kapong (*Tetrameles nudiflora*), with its flanged buttresses, is another tall tree here. These forests abound with epiphytes, including many ferns and orchids. Palms such as *Calamus* and *Caryota* are also locally abundant. More than 4,000 species of higher plants have been recorded here, more than 100 mammal species and about 425 birds, including specialities such as green peafowl, Hume's pheasant and rufous-necked hornbill (*Aceros nipalensis*), more than 60 reptiles and 38 amphibians. The insects are fascinating too, especially the butterflies, notably several species of swallowtail.

One spot, Yexianggu (Wild Elephant Valley) near Mengyang, has been developed for tourists to spot elephants. This broad forested valley of about 670ha hosts gaur and peacocks as well as the famous elephants, which can be seen (with luck) from a purpose-built overhead walkway. Tourists are also 'entertained' by trained elephants nearby.

Nonggang NR (Guangxi) is a relatively small yet very rich reserve near the border with Vietnam, featuring karst country, with limestone subtropical broadleaf evergreen forest. Notable species here are white-headed leaf monkey, rhesus and Assamese macaques, Malayan night heron, Oriental hobby, red junglefowl, Oriental pied hornbill, babblers, spiderhunters and white-winged magpie. Further south is the much larger and relatively unexplored reserve of **Shiwandashan NR** (Guangxi), protecting 1,745 km^2 of lowland and hill tropical forest, rich in figs, bamboos and palms. Mammals include Asian wild dog, clouded leopard and Chinese goral. Notable birds are white-eared night heron, Oriental dwarf kingfisher, red-headed trogon and owlets. Black-throated laughingthrush is common here.

Neilingding-Futian NR (Guangdong). Neilingding is an island in the Pearl River, best known for its colony of rhesus macaques, while Futian is an area of mangroves opposite Mai Po. Wetland birds include black-faced spoonbill, Chinese egret and Dalmatian pelican. **Zhujiangkou NR** (Guangdong) is another Pearl River reserve, protecting the estuary habitat of the rare pink Chinese dolphin.

Huidonggang Sea Turtle NR (Guangdong), further up the coast to the east, conserves breeding colonies of green turtles. The sandy beaches support about 500 turtles at egg-laying time.

Mai Po Marshes NR (Hong Kong) is a famous wetland reserve. The best tidal reserve in southeast China, it has mudflats, mangroves, shrimp ponds and reedbeds, and attracts large numbers of migrant birds including rarities. The best time to visit is April for migration, and at this time there can be a staggering 40 species of wader present as well as masses of migrant songbirds (especially in the casuarina bushes). In winter the waterfowl are impressive, with black-faced spoonbill and Dalmatian pelican.

Rhesus macaque monkeys drinking on Nanwan Monkey Island, off Hainan Island.

The island of **Hainan** has several important reserves, some coastal, protecting coral reefs, others inland, protecting hill forest. September through January is the driest period.

Datian NR (Hainan) in the west is rather dry, with savanna-forest and grassland, and is noted for its population of Eld's deer, endemic to Hainan and now numbering more than 1,000, increased from only 26 in 1976. Red junglefowl is quite common. Further inland, **Bawangling NR** (Hainan) has rich tropical broadleaf hill forest, with clouded leopard, Asiatic black bear, black giant squirrel, red and white giant flying squirrel (*Petaurista alborufus*) and Hainan black gibbon (*Hylobates (Nomascus) nasutus hainanus*). The gibbon is now endemic to Hainan with fewer than 20 individuals left in the world. The nominate subspecies (*N. n. nasutus*) occurs in northeast Vietnam, in a comparably tiny population.

The birds are very good here and include Hainan partridge, silver pheasant, Hainan leaf warbler and white-winged magpie (*Urocissa whiteheadi*). Due south of Datian is **Jianfengling NR** (Hainan), which is one of the more accessible reserves. The main habitats are broadleaf evergreen tropical, palm-rich hill forests, and dwarf mountain forest at higher levels. Notable species include rhesus macaque, leopard cat, flying squirrels, ratchet-tailed treepie, white-winged magpie, rufous-cheeked laughingthrush, Hainan leaf warbler and yellow-billed nuthatch. Right in the centre is **Wuzhishan NR** (Hainan), the island's largest reserve, mainly hill and montane forest on the slopes of Hainan's highest peak (1,864m). Notable species here are Hainan partridge, green and mountain imperial pigeons, Oriental dwarf kingfisher, rufous-cheeked laughingthrush, Hainan leaf warbler, yellow-billed nuthatch (*Sitta solangiae*) and drongos. **Nanwanmihou NR** (Hainan) protects an area of coastal hills in the southeast of the island, which has rhesus macaques. **Sanyashanhujiao NR** (Hainan) is a marine reserve protecting part of Hainan's coral reefs.

FURTHER READING

Angel, H, *Giant Pandas*, Evans Mitchell Books, Rickmansworth, 2006

Chapman, G P and Wang, Y-Z, *The Plant Life of China*, Springer, Berlin, 2002

Evans, T, *Great Wall of China*, Bradt Travel Guides, 2006

Gosney, D, *Birding in China* (DVD), Gostours, 2007

He Shan-an, *Rare and Precious Plants of China*, Shanghai Scientific and Technical Publishers, Shanghai, 1998

Ji Weizhi, *Wildlife in Yunnan*, China Forestry Publishing House, Kunming, 1999

Laidler, L and Laidler, K, *China's Threatened Wildlife*, Blandford, London, 1996

MacKinnon, J, *Wild China*, New Holland, London, 1999

MacKinnon, J and Phillipps, K *A, Field Guide to the Birds of China*, Oxford University Press, Oxford, 2000

MacKinnon J M, Sha M, Cheung C, Carey G, Xiang Z and Melville D, *A biodiversity review of China*, World Wide Fund for Nature, Hong Kong, 1996

Valder, P, *Gardens in China*, Timber Press, Oregon, 2002

Viney, C Phillips, K and Ying, Lam Chiu, *The Birds of Hong Kong and South China*, Hong Kong Government Information Service, 2005

Woodward, T, *Birding South-East China*, Tim Woodward, Hong Kong, 2006

Xu Zhihui (editor in chief), *Natural Museum – Nature Reserves in Yunnan*, Yunnan University Press, Kunming, 1999

Zhao, J (ed), Zheng Guangmei, Wang Huadong, Xu Jialin, *The Natural History of China*, McGraw Hill Publishing Company, New York, 1990

Walters, M, *China: Yunnan Province*, Bradt Travel Guides, 2007

For those with a serious interest in China's plants, the best English resource is the splendid Flora of China project, accessible online at http://flora.huh.harvard.edu/china.